LONG LIVE THE HODAG!

LONG LIVE THE HODAG!

The Life and Legacy of Eugene Simeon Shepard: 1854-1923

by

Kurt Daniel Kortenhof

Hodag Press®

Publication Data:

Kortenhof, Kurt Daniel, 1971-
Long Live the Hodag! The Life and Legacy of Eugene Simeon
Shepard, 1854-1923
Includes bibliographical references.
1. Shepard, Eugene Simeon, 1854-1923
2. Rhinelander, WI - History - Community
Boosterism - Hodag
3. Wisconsin - History - Folklore - Hodag
4. Midwest - History - Lumbering - Land Trade
I. Title.

ISBN 0-9653745-0-5

Hodag Press®
5552 Jenny Webber Lake Road
Rhinelander, Wisconsin 54501

PREFACE

During the summer of 1995 I renewed my interest in Midwestern regional history and began reading books on lumbering, the land trade, and Wisconsin history in general. I continually ran across brief references to Eugene Shepard and his 1896 "capture" of the Rhinelander hodag. Having spent most of my 24 years living near Rhinelander, I became increasingly interested in the hodag and the person who brought the fictional beast to life. Knowing that the hodag still plays a prominent role in Rhinelander, and realizing that the following year marked the centennial of its "capture," I thought it would be of some use to write a brief history of the beast, no more than fifteen pages, and send it to the city's district library and chamber of commerce. With that admittedly modest goal, I began collecting notes from secondary sources and consulting late nineteenth-century city newspapers. Almost immediately I discovered that Eugene Shepard left behind an unusually colorful, and relatively accessible, historical record.

As the summer drew to a close and I prepared to begin my final year as a history student at the University of Wisconsin-Eau Claire, my project had expanded. I successfully submitted my preliminary research to Dr. Louise Edwards-Simpson as a proposal for a graduate research paper. Unable to complete even the first section of my proposed paper within the confines of one semester, I decided to expand my project once again. By late November of 1995, what I had originally envisioned as a fifteen-page paper had evolved into the topic of my master's thesis.

Although the way I envisioned this study continually expanded, my understanding of its audience always remained constant. I wrote *Long Live the Hodag!* for a general audience - for those interested in Rhinelander's past, regional history and Northern Wisconsin folklore. It is my hope that those who endeavor to read the following pages learn about Eugene Shepard and his hodag and grasp more fully the significance of this important piece of Rhinelander's local color. It is also my hope, however, that those same readers learn a bit more about regional history and the development of turn-of-the-century Northern Wisconsin as it is illustrated through the experiences of Eugene Shepard.

Although I take sole responsibility for the errors that may appear in the following pages, the credit for what is correct (or as near to correct as possible) must be shared. Many people have given me assistance throughout every stage of this study. A grant I received from the College of Professional Studies and University Research at the University of Wisconsin-Eau Claire made several trips to Rhinelander, Antigo and Star Lake possible. This grant also covered essential expenses such as purchasing supplies, taking and developing photographs and photo-copying. Many professors at the University of Wisconsin-Eau Claire became involved in this project and their insightful critiques enhanced this study greatly. I am indebted to Dr. Louise Edwards-Simpson, Dr. James W. Oberly, Dr. Robert J. Gough, Dr. Maxwell P. Schoenfeld, Dr. Ronald A. Warloski and Dr. Wil Denson. Dave Peterson, author of *Hodag! A New Musical*, graciously help me acquire a copy of his 1964 play script from the Mills Music Library at the University of Wisconsin-Madison. Matt Rowe, an old roommate and friend, lent much-appreciated assistance by proofreading an early draft of my manuscript. My sister, Kim Kortenhof, edtited the final draft of my manuscript and greatly improved the finished product.

In addition to the above mentioned, many people in and associated with Rhinelander and Northern Wisconsin also helped make this study possible. The staffs at the Rhinelander District Library and the Oneida County Clerk of Court Office made available various essential resources and aided me in the research phase of this study. Alice and Mary Louise Rismon gave me valuable insight into Shepard's involvement in the development of Star Lake, Wisconsin. Likewise, Joan Belongia-Mode assisted me in this area by lending me several books on Star Lake, Wisconsin history. Phone interviews with Margery Peters of Rhinelander, a lifelong friend of the Shepard family, and Mary Kosloske of Winchester, Virginia, the granddaughter of Eugene S. Shepard, gave colorful insight that other sources unavoidably lacked. Finally, two of Rhinelander's local historians not only shared my interest and excitement for this topic, but gladly gave me unmeasurable assistance. I sincerely thank Lee Mayer and Joy Vancos for their assistance, insight and friendship.

At this point, *Long Live the Hodag!* represents the capstone of my education. I would not have been able to take advantage of this education if it were not for the support and encouragement of my parents, Nancy and Steve Kortenhot, Jr. Not only did they invest a great deal of financial resources in my future, but they took a genuine interest in my educational goals. For this and many other things too numerous to list, I dedicate *Long Live The Hodag!* to my mother and father with my sincere thanks and my warmest appreciation. -KDK

Eau Claire, Wisconsin
June, 1996.

CONTENTS

FIGURES

INTRODUCTION

Shortly after noon on March 30, 1923, a horse-drawn hearse trudged through the streets of Rhinelander, Wisconsin. An unusually fierce spring storm had buried the Northern Wisconsin city in snow that morning, and only after some difficulty did the hearse arrive at its destination: a residence known as "The Pines," just south of the city proper. The funeral service was held at the home of the deceased under the auspices of the Masonic Lodge of Rhinelander. Before proceeding to Forest Home Cemetery, the horses, blocked in the narrow driveway by funeral goers, had to be unhitched from the hearse, the shoveled area of the driveway expanded, and the hearse turned around. This was a difficult task in the bitter cold, high winds and blowing snow of the waning storm.[1]

Upon arrival at the cemetery the winds began to pick up in uneven gusts, and snow continued to fall as Alex McRae, one of Rhinelander's leading citizens, read from the Bible. An umbrella was taken by the wind and

---

[1] Eye-witness account of E.S Shepard's funeral recounted by John Remo as quoted in: Robert E. Gard and L.G. Sorden, Wisconsin Lore (Sauk City, Wisconsin, 1976), 259-60; "Rhinelander Pioneer Dies," Rhinelander Daily News, March 27, 1923, p.1; "Shepard Rites at the Pines," Rhinelander Daily News, March 31, 1923, p.1; "Life Closes for E.S. Shepard," New North (Rhinelander, Wisconsin), March 29, 1923, p.1; Eugene S. Shepard, Death Certificate c-1 830 #601, March 24, 1923. Oneida County, Wisconsin.

fluttered away as the funeral director prepared to lower the casket into the grave. The machine-driven device recently purchased by the funeral home to lower caskets into the graves stalled after lowering the coffin only a foot. Attempting to repair the machine, the operator collapsed a side of the grave and fell into the opening. The congregation snickered and an embarrassed laugh escaped. John Reno, in attendance at the funeral, believed he heard even the deceased laughing at the mishaps. In 1923 March truly "went out like a lion," and so too did Rhinelander's most eccentric and notable citizen, Eugene S. Shepard.[2]

In many ways Shepard's funeral epitomized his life: unique, difficult and humorous. Shepard is remembered for his humor as it relates to Rhinelander and lumberjack lore. His most famous accomplishment, the popularization of the hodag, a fictional lizard-like beast "captured" near Rhinelander, Wisconsin in 1896, has been recounted in newspapers from Bangor, Maine to Fairbanks, Alaska. In fact, it is difficult to find a book focusing on Northern Wisconsin history, lumbering, or regional lore that does not offer some discussion of E.S. Shepard and his capture of the hodag. Unfortunately, these accounts are extremely brief, incomplete, and often inconsistent. The capture and ensuing legend of the hodag has not been investigated and evaluated in a detailed fashion. In addition, other aspects of Shepard's life have been widely ignored.[3]

----

[2] Gard, <u>Wisconsin Lore</u>, 259-60.

[3] For a survey of secondary literature regarding Shepard's capture of the Hodag and other pranks see: Robert E. Gard, and L.G. Sorden, <u>Wisconsin Lore</u> (Sauk City, Wisconsin, 1976), pp. 73, 245-61; Gerald Carlstein, "The Beast That Will Not Die," <u>Wisconsin Trails</u> 20:2, August 1979, p. 29-30; "Hoax Alive and Well: Hodag Fooled Some People For A Time," <u>Wisconsin Then and Now</u>, 22:1, August 1975; Jack Cory, <u>Jack Cory's Scrapbook</u> (Lake Tomahawk, Wisconsin, 1985), pp. 5-7; August Derleth, <u>The Wisconsin: River of a Thousand Isles</u> (Madison, Wisconsin, 1942), pp. 190, 207-12;

An investigation of E.S. Shepard's life (1854-1923) reveals much more than the origin of the Rhinelander hodag. Shepard performed many roles: farm hand, sought-after timber cruiser, resident land speculator, surveyor, map maker, business entrepreneur, amateur artist, writer, poet, editor, and resort operator. He held several government offices and became active in state politics; he was fluent in the Ojibwa (Chippewa) language and sought to educate others in regard to the Ojibwa culture; he loved nature and created a wildlife preserve; he worked to advance the settlement and development of Rhinelander; and he was, to be sure, a practical joker.

Shepard was an intelligent man who could recognize the opportunities Northern Wisconsin had to offer. He also, however, allowed himself to enter into questionable business endeavors and to overlook obvious impossibilities which often resulted in financial setbacks. Shepard endured other problems as well; he often drank to excess and he eventually found himself alienated from both his family and, toward the end of his life, from society in general. The uniqueness of Shepard's character (negative attributes as well as positive) and breadth of his experience offer insight into various aspects of turn-of-the-century Northern Wisconsin history.

This biography of Eugene Shepard focuses on three interconnected themes: Shepard's role in the Midwestern land trade, his involvement in community boosterism and

Fred L. Holmes, Badger Saints and Sinners (Milwaukee, Wisconsin, 1938), pp. 459-74; Luke S. Kearney, The Hodag: and Other Tales of the Logging Camps (Madison, Wisconsin, 1928), pp. 3-28; Curtis D. MacDougall, Hoaxes (New York, 1921), pp. 17-18; T.V. Olsen, Our First Hundred Years: A History of Rhinelander (Rhinelander, Wisconsin, 1981), pp. 95-105; T.V. Olsen, The Rhinelander Country Volume Two: Birth of a City (Rhinelander, Wisconsin, 1983), pp. 35-36, 64, 113, 122-23, 128, 136-37, 139; David Peterson, Hodag: A New Musical (Madison, 1964); William F. Stark, Wisconsin, River of History (1988), pp. 244-49.

his eccentric personality. The first theme studies the role of the timber cruiser, local land agent and resident land speculator as the lumber industry harvested the Midwest's timber. The second theme relates to the development of Rhinelander as a logging boomtown and its perpetuation as a regional industrial center. This transition is studied within the context of the significant role Shepard played in the city's development through active participation in local government and extensive involvement in voluntary booster organizations. Rhinelander offers an interesting case study of the process of industrial diversification as the city faced the rapid decline of the lumber trade. The third theme focuses on Shepard's personality, and in particular his creativity, humor, and familiarity with lumberjack lore. His personality traits tie the first two themes together; he employed his talents in his work as a timber cruiser and businessman, and in his endeavors to promote Rhinelander. Ultimately, these traits resulted in Shepard's weighty contribution to lumberjack lore.

Eugene Simeon Shepard was born in Old Fort Howard (present-day Green Bay, Wisconsin) on March 22, 1854. Shortly thereafter his father, Simeon Shepard, moved his family to New London, Waupaca County, Wisconsin. Eugene received a sixth grade education in New London schools, and he spent much of his youth working on his father's farm. In 1866, Simeon Shepard died and Eugene, at age twelve, was "thrown upon his own resources." He initially began working as a hired hand on several New London farms, and, for a short period, he piloted a tug boat along the Wolf River. By 1870, the youthful Shepard found his vocation in the woods of Northern Wisconsin where he served as an apprentice on a land-hunting expedition. On September 9, 1876, Eugene, age 23, wed Mildred "Molly" Woodworth, two years his junior and the daughter of Captain Sidney and Alice Woodworth, a prominent New London family. The following year the couple had their first son, Claude. Layton, Claude's only sibling, was born fifteen years later in 1892.[4]

It was six years before his marriage that Shepard found his calling in life. In 1870, a group of wealthy eastern land speculators hired Albert A. Webber, an experienced New London timber assessor, to inspect the pine stands of the upper Wisconsin River Valley. Webber hired the sixteen-year-old Shepard as an assistant, and he introduced the latter to the art of timber cruising or "land looking." From this introduction, Shepard became one of the most sought-after timber cruisers in the upper Middle West.[5]

In addition to providing him an apprenticeship in his eventual trade, Shepard's initial cruising trip also introduced him to the upper Wisconsin River Valley. On their return south from land looking in the vicinity of Eagle River, Webber and Shepard camped at the confluence of the Pelican and Wisconsin Rivers. In 1870, the location (approximately 45 miles due north of present-day Wausau) was known as Pelican Rapids; it later became the city of

---

[4] Holmes, Badger Saints and Sinners, 460; Olsen, Birth of a City, 35; United States Federal Census, New London, Waupaca County, Wisconsin, 1880; United States Federal Census, Arbor Vita, Vilas County, Wisconsin, 1900; "Mrs. Shepard is Taken by Death," Rhinelander Daily News, December 26, 1925, p.1; A.T. Andreas, Compiler, History of Northern Wisconsin: Containing an Account of its Settlement, Growth, Development and Resources... (Chicago, 1881), 1095; Mary Shepard Kosloske of Winchester, Virginia, interviewed by author, 29 February, 1996, Telephone call from Eau Claire Wisconsin to Winchester, Virginia. Mary Kosloske is E.S. Shepard's granddaughter.

[5] Eugene Shepard, "Reminiscences of Eugene Shepard: Old and Well Known Citizen First Came Here Away Back in 1870," New North (Rhinelander, Wisconsin), December 12, 1912. The December 12, 1912 issue of the New North is the thirtieth anniversary issue of the paper. The edition is expanded and features numerous stories written by pioneer citizens focusing on the origin and history of the city.

Rhinelander. The city was founded in 1882 and Shepard was on hand to witness its first half year. In 1886 Shepard made Rhinelander his permanent home. Several years before the men most responsible for the establishment of Rhinelander set foot in the vicinity, and twelve years before the city was platted, E.S. Shepard looked over the natural advantages of the location. Forty-two years later, Shepard recalled his first impressions of the site that eventually became the seat of Oneida County:

> I came down and explored the flat country where the city now stands. The land was covered with a thick growth of jack pine and larger long slim Norway. Mr. John C. Curran had settled at the mouth of the Pelican river [*sic*] some 16 years before and had a clearing made where the city park [Shepard Park] now stands. He was engaged [in] buying furs from the Indians and in a small way logging in company with L.S. Coon of Wausau and Berlin. A dozen yoke of oxen were grazing around the country and about a dozen families of Indians lived in tepees around the place and worked as Indians usually do at intervals.[6]

From this point onward, Eugene S. Shepard became intimately involved with the development of Northern Wisconsin in general and Rhinelander in particular.

---

[6] Shepard, "Reminisces," New North, December 12, 1912. T.V. Olsen notes that Shepard had over estimated the time Curran had lived at Pelican Rapids, stating he had lived there 11 years not 16, See: Olsen, Birth of a City, 35.

Figure 1.1: Eugene S. Shepard, circa 1876.
Rhinelander District Library Collection.

Figure 1.2: Eugene S. Shepard and his Hodag.
Drawing by Lee Mayer, 1991.

CHAPTER I

"THE PINE LAND MAN"

As the proliferation of rail transport opened new stands of pine and hardwoods to the lumber industry, Eugene Shepard entered upon his apprenticeship in the timber-cruising trade. Timber cruisers, according to Paul W. Gates, were "an important class on the pine-land frontier. They were employed by capitalists, lumbermen and agents to cruise timbered sections and to estimate the amount of pine timber of the size in commercial demand." The federal land policy, absentee land speculators and the booming lumber industry produced a vast market for such men and required the refinement of skills associated with their job. The need for land and timber assessors, however, was as old as America itself.[1]

Beginning with European colonization, through Frederick Jackson Turner's "Frontier Thesis," to recent environmental interpretations of American history, the conception and understanding of America was and is closely associated with the value of her natural resources. One of the most obvious and easiest resources to exploit is timber. From the earliest days of Anglo-America, Royal Assessors traveled through the wooded areas of New England marking suitable trees with the King's seal. These

---

[1] Paul W. Gates, The Wisconsin Pine Lands of Cornell University: A Study in Land Policy and Absentee Ownership (Ithaca, New York, 1943), 92.

trees were reserved for the use of the Royal Navy, and the best of them became the masts of His Majesty's Ships. American ship building and exportation of processed lumber quickly became a major industry, and the woods of America were exploited.

Just as Royal Assessors completed the first step in the processing of virgin forests for ships and masts, every utilization of timber began with some type of assessment. Most often this assessment was completed by a representative, or someone in the employ of, the person or company that eventually reaped the benefit of the finished product. As such, the art of timber assessing, timber cruising, timber estimating, land hunting, or land looking played a crucial role in the lumber industry and became a profitable occupation for America's young, adventurous and energetic men.[2]

By the second half of the nineteenth century, the ill-advised public land policies of the federal government and the lumber industry's need to exploit the Midwest's timber resources clashed. This combination bred a corrupt system of land transfer that pitted absentee land speculators against large lumber companies with local land agents and timber cruisers acting as middlemen.

Federal land policy was, from its origin, characterized by conflict between speculators wishing to acquire large tracts of land for future profit, and homesteaders wishing to acquire affordable small parcels of government land on which to settle. The government, in need of the revenue that large land sales brought, traditionally ruled on the side of the land speculators. By the mid-nineteenth century, however, that policy underwent meaningful agrarian reform. This reform culminated in the

---

[2] For recent environmental interpretations of American history see: William Cronan, Changes in the Land: Indians, Colonists, and the Ecology of New England (New York, 1983), and Nature's Metropolis: Chicago and the Great West (New York, 1991).

passage of the 1862 Homestead Act, which provided grants of 160 acres to actual settlers. Despite these changes, large tracts of land in Wisconsin and elsewhere continued to fall into the hands of absentee speculators. Additionally, the government, wishing to foster rapid growth of the country's infrastructure, continually granted public lands "to aid schools, highways, canals, railroads and other public institutions." These lands, although invested for public good in different areas of the country, were nonetheless owned by absentee speculators.[3]

In the simplest terms, land speculators purchased large parcels of public land immediately prior to the emergence of real demand (i.e., immigration and settlement or the lumber industry). In most cases the purchases were made at the government-established minimum price of $1.25 per acre. The speculators then held their investment until the demand for, and value of, the lands rose. Barring any economic downturn or excessive taxes, the speculators could turn a profit. In Wisconsin's largest and most celebrated example, Cornell University netted over five million dollars by manipulating the Agricultural College Act and investing in Wisconsin's pine lands. Land speculation in Wisconsin was not a sure thing, however, and the economy and local taxation became the downfall of many absentee speculators. Cornell University was, if anything, the exception to the rule. To be successful in Midwest land speculation, eastern investors had to manage their affairs with the utmost care and craft. Most important was to acquire an accurate assessment of the lands they were purchasing and selling. They also needed to protect their investments from timber thieving lumber companies, protest excessive taxation and pay unavoidable taxes promptly. To accomplish these necessities, the speculators

[3] Gates, The Wisconsin Pine Lands of Cornell University, 1-2.

relied on local agents and timber cruisers.[4]

As logging companies began to exploit the Midwest and purchase large tracts from the government or land speculators, they too relied on the services of the timber cruisers. If a lumber company wished to purchase a tract of pine land from an absentee speculator, it first sent land lookers to acquire a detailed estimate of the value of the timber. The speculator, if not in the possession of a cruiser's report beforehand, sent his own cruisers to acquire the information. The actions of both purchaser and seller were defined by the confidential reports of the woodsmen they employed. By the nineteenth century, as the lumber companies began to tap Wisconsin's pineries, they were growing in size and wealth. The land transactions they entered into with the government or eastern speculators became extremely large and involved huge sums of money. Consequently, the role of the timber assessors became more important; the services required became more detailed and specific. As a result, the need for competent, accurate and honest men became a paramount concern of land speculators and lumber companies.[5]

By mid-century a window emerged that denoted an interesting period in the role of timber cruisers. The importance of their craft required the men to acquire an extraordinary skill, and technology had not yet made the cruisers obsolete or even eased the burden of their work. Furthermore, forestry schools that would soon produce university-trained forestry professionals had not yet fully emerged. From 1850-1920, the role of the woodsman land lookers reached its apex. By the 1920s the adoption of developing technology greatly altered the role of the timber

---

[4] Ibid., 242-43.

[5] J.C. Ryan, "The Timber Cruisers," Timber Bulletin, 47 (April/May, 1992), pp. 27-28.

assessors. Not only did it fundamentally change the occupation, but it assumed that timber assessors had the scientific skills acquired through a structured educational program. By 1925 the role of the old-style woodsman/timber estimator had been eclipsed by technology and the emergence of college-educated foresters.[6]

Nineteenth- and early twentieth-century timber cruisers had to travel by water, dog sled or foot into the land they evaluated. Embarking on tours often longer than six months, the cruisers had to carry all of their essential tools and utensils. In black knapsacks or strapped blanketed packs, a cruiser carried cooking utensils, axes, maps, plats, field notebooks, surveying tools, tents, blankets, and dried provisions (including flour, meat, beans, coffee, sugar, rice, pepper and salt). Depending on the individual and the length of trip, cruisers carried 50 to 100 lbs. of tools and provisions.

In addition to the burden of carrying all the essential tools of the trade, timber cruisers faced numerous other difficulties. Setting up and breaking camp daily in the summers, and several times per week in the winters, was a necessary and difficult task. Leaving camp for his daily cruising venture was filled with even greater hardships, however. Traveling up rivers against strong currents, crossing lakes in birch-bark canoes, facing high winds and rain, fording streams without boat or bridge, constructing rafts to cross larger rivers and lakes, and traversing miles of swamps all had to be accomplished while estimating and noting timber qualities. Furthermore, extreme heat and swarming insects in the summers and bitter-cold temperatures in the winters made a certain part of the

---

[6] For short discussions of technological advances and the "end of an era," see: Donald Mackay, The Lumberjacks (Toronto, 1978), 68-72; and J.C. Ryan "The Forgotten Cruiser," Timber Bulletin, 40 (Aug/Sept) 1992, p. 31.

timber cruiser's duty miserable.[7]

Possibly more distressing than physical hardships were those of mental anxiety caused by separation from society and family. Cruisers were cut off not only from news of civilization, but, more importantly, from word of loved ones. This situation often lasted months. George Warren, cruising in the vicinity of the Boundary Waters of Minnesota during the winter of 1874-75, vividly described this situation:

> No letters nor communications of any kind reached us after winter set in, until our arrival at Grand Rapids in the month of February following....I had left my young wife and infant daughter, not yet a year old, in Minneapolis. Either, or both might have died and been buried before any word could have reached me. It was not possible at all times to keep such thoughts out of my mind.[8]

The impossibility of knowing when the opportunity to mail

---

[7] Ryan, "The Forgotten Cruiser," 31; Mackay, The Lumberjacks, 62; George Henry Warren, The Pioneer Woodsman As He Relates To Lumbering in the Northwest (Minneapolis, 1914), 47.
        The bulk of this information is paraphrased from Warren. Of the insects that hampered the cruisers, the black fly is most often mentioned. Swarming in mass numbers in the heat of the summers they congregated in areas recently devastated by forest fires (a situation that required cruisers to evaluate the extent and character of the damage). Black fly bites cause swelling and welting of the skin; the fly had a intolerable ability to infiltrate clothing and hair. Warren, after cruising a recently burned tract in northern Wisconsin, returned to his hotel in Wausau. Although he was well known by the owner and employees, he was not recognized and mistakenly taken for a victim of small-pox on account of the damage the black flies had done to his appearance. Bacon grease rubbed liberally into the skin was the best protection Warren found to ward off such insects. See: Warren, The Pioneer Woodsman, 160-65.

[8] Warren, The Pioneer Woodsman, 120.

a letter would arrive caused additional anxiety. The status of letters sent, most often by the most awkward and uncertain means, was also impossible to know. Cruisers could never be certain that letters they sent ever reached their destination. Warren recalled:

> Letters were occasionally written and kept in readiness to send out by any Indian who might be going to the nearest lumber camp, whence they might by chance be carried out to some post office. Whether these letters reached their destinations or not, could not be known by the writers as long as they remained in their work, hidden in the forest.[9]

Shepard was on an extended cruising trip in the same area over fifteen years later. Although the mail system had improved by late 1891, Shepard noted that it was still crude, difficult and uncertain: "I have to row about thirty miles to mail this. Our mail is carried by a four tandem dog team with a half-breed driver and toboggan. It comes twice every month.... So I have not heard from home for several months, but suppose my folks are well."[10]

The difficulties of the trade were accompanied by very real dangers. The forests were full of hidden pitfalls that could result in an injury severe enough to cause death in the absence of medical attention. Tripping over a hidden stump or log could result in breaking a limb or striking one's head and falling unconscious. Either situation could be very difficult when alone in the woods, often hundreds of miles away from any assistance. Traversing rapidly moving rivers and swamps of unknown character was equally dangerous.

The unpredictable nature of wild animals, particularly bears and wolves, also added to the dangers of

---

[9] Ibid., 120.

[10] Eugene S. Shepard, "Big Fork Country," New North, December 17, 1891, p.1.

the woodsman's trade. On a trip late in 1891, Shepard rescued his mentor and cruising partner, A.A. Webber, from an altercation with a bear. Webber had gotten too close to the animal's cubs, and the bear had chased him up a tree. Shepard, reaching Webber just in time, killed the bear. Writing from the same trip, Shepard made another reference to the dangers of wild animals to the cruiser. In closing his letter Shepard half jokingly stated: "if the wolves leave me alone I will get through all o.k."[11]

Winter, a season that saw increased cruising activity due to the ease of travel, increased the dangers involved in timber cruising. The bitter-cold temperature and ferocious windchill that characterize the Middle West during the winter months added an additional element of danger to the occupation. Crossing unfamiliar waterways was perhaps the most dangerous situation cruisers faced during winter. Heavy snow often hid natural springs that were covered by only a thin layer of ice. Falling through the ice caused devastation. A woodsman lost much of his equipment, and often his field notes, in such situations. Far more serious, however, was the inability of some to pull themselves from the freezing water. Already restricting heavy clothes often became unmanageable when water logged. When added to the shock of submerging in freezing water, falling through the ice often proved too much to overcome. If the woodsman was fortunate enough to escape the water, he was then in danger of hyperthermia. This situation only prolonged the inevitable.[12]

These dangers, along with the increased demands on cruisers, resulted in the creation of cruising crews.

---

[11] Warren, The Pioneer Woodsman, 113-115; Ryan, "The Forgotten Cruiser," 30; Mackay, The Lumberjacks, 60-62; Shepard "Big Fork Country," New North, December 17, 1891.

[12] Mackay, The Lumberjacks, 60-61; Warren, The Pioneer Woodsman, 113-14; Ryan, "The Forgotten Cruiser," 30-31.

Originally it was common for cruisers to work alone, but by the time Shepard entered the trade it was an unwritten rule that one should not enter the woods alone. Notices printed in Rhinelander's first weekly, the *New North*, of men found dead in the woods by lumber companies served as a constant reminder to woodsmen of the dangers inherent in the woods. When A.A. Webber hired Shepard in 1870, he did so as much for safety as he did for assistance. Webber apparently gave Shepard a broad range of responsibilities that embraced all aspects of the cruising trade. Shepard recalled that Webber "made a cruiser, cook, compass man, beast of burden and canoe man of him." Although this arrangement of two-man crews was probably very common, most cruising crews were larger, with a more defined separation of duties. This became the organization of many of the crews Eugene Shepard later led.[13]

Cruising crews ranged in size and definition from two-man operations like the Webber-Shepard expedition in 1870 up through twenty-man crews that cruised the Canadian forests in the early twentieth century. During the late nineteenth century the average cruising crew employed in the Midwest consisted of three to seven men. In most cases men acquired strictly defined skills that coincided with specific duties. The three most common divisions were the appraiser or crew leader, compass man, and cook. The appraiser and compass man engaged in conducting the actual appraising. The compass man "ran the compass," and blazed a trail which the appraiser followed while estimating the usable timber. The cook was responsible for establishing and breaking camp and providing food for the crew. As crews became more elaborate and the techniques of the cruisers became more detailed other positions were added. A good example was the addition of a "calibrator," who traveled with the crews sampling tree diameters and

[13]   Shepard, "Reminiscences," <u>New North</u>, December 12, 1912.

drilling plugs to sample age.[14]

There were two types of cruising assignments. The first involved locating large tracts of timber stands. This required a definition of the general characteristics of the land: location, rough size, logging possibilities, and access to rivers and lakes. This type of cruising was the less detailed and technical of the two, and it was often done before the land was even surveyed by the government. Its goal was to provide the employer with a general idea of the type and extent of timber that lay over a large area. On occasion these trips engaged the cruiser for the better part of a year and led him over vast distances. By the turn of the century most of the large tracts in the Middle West were cruised, surveyed, and sold. As a result, this type of job became a thing of the past.[15]

The second type of assignment required cruisers to provide a detailed report of the timber on a particular parcel. Parcels ranged in size from 40 acres to entire townships of 6 miles square. This assignment required a highly technical and detailed survey of the tract in question. The cruiser had the ability to estimate with startling accuracy the amount of board feet of lumber that could be taken from the parcel. Individual methods for this estimation process were unique to the woodsman, but every cruiser used some variation of sample stripping. "Horse-shoeing," for example, required two runs through a forty-acre section. Since this was a fairly small area, a cruiser could get a good idea of what the forty contained from just two passes. Running a compass line or strip through a

---

[14] Ryan, "The Forgotten Cruiser," 30-31; Mackay, The Lumberjacks, 62-63. This job specification is only one example of the actual character of these crews. It is clear, however, that this division was fairly common. If crews consisted of only two people the job distinction was less definite, and the assistant most often acted as a jack of all trades (as Shepard did for Webber).

[15] Ryan, "The Timber Cruiser," 27.

slightly larger tract of land was also a common practice. As the cruiser walked his compass line, he estimated and recorded in his field notes the number and size of the logs that could be cut from each tree. Several other compass lines, running parallel to the first and often separated by less than a half mile, were surveyed, estimated and noted. From the light of a campfire the cruiser calculated the potential yield of the tract during the following evening.[16]

Government surveys, conducted before the lands were put on the market, made locating tracts to be cruised much easier. This survey made the second type of cruising assignment possible. The Continental Congress Land Ordinance of 1785 developed and dictated a system of surveying government lands. The ordinance required the establishment of "Range Lines," parallel lines six miles apart running north and south, and "township lines," parallel lines six miles apart running east and west. Each six-mile-square section defined a township and was denoted by a numerical system. Two lines of reference standardized the system: a base line as an orientation for the range lines, and a meridian line as an orientation for the township lines. Townships were further divided by five parallel lines running north and south, and five running east and west. This created thirty-six sections of one square mile.[17]

Government surveyors, many of whom later became private timber cruisers and land agents, were employed to execute the survey. The surveyors marked each township corner with a post displaying the range and township numbers of the intersection. The marked portion of the post faced a "bearing tree" in the corner of the township

[16] Ibid., 28; Mackay, The Lumberjacks, 55, 62-63.

[17] Robert C. Nesbit, Wisconsin: A History, 2nd ed. (Madison, Wisconsin, 1989) 135; Warren, The Pioneer Woodsman, 22-24.

which bore the same markings. The sections were denoted in the same fashion. In addition, "quarter corners" marked the median of every one-mile side of a section. Physical descriptions of bearing trees accompanied by detailed maps were placed on record at the Land Office in Washington D.C. As a result, with the existence of only one bearing tree or marking post, used in conjunction with government supplied plat books and field notes (acquired at the local land office), a cruiser could easily locate particular townships and sections. By running parallel lines connecting the quarter markers, timber cruisers divided the one-mile sections into four 160-acre subdivisions. Repeating the process yielded forty-acre sections. These divisions, referred to as "forties," remain the smallest regular governmental subdivisions. These townships, 160-acre subdivisions, and forties provided a grid for the location of cruising assignments.[18]

Upon completion of the surveys, the President placed the lands on the market by holding a public auction. The government advertised these auctions in advance and land speculators and lumber companies employed timber cruisers to inspect the land and provide the buyers with "descriptions" of the land they deemed profitable. Bidding began at $1.25 per acre, and most land was purchased at the minimum price. Land not sold during the auction was open to purchase thereafter. The northern sections of the Wisconsin and Chippewa River Valleys were surveyed and put up for auction in 1866, but they were not purchased due to concerns over ease of access. Lands not acquired at the auction, but desired afterward, were then open to purchase. Federal land had to be purchased in local land offices, and that belonging to the state of Wisconsin had to

[18] Nesbit, Wisconsin: A History, 142; Warren, The Pioneer Woodsman, 22-25.

be purchased at Madison.[19]

This process of acquiring government lands created a competitive situation for the timber cruisers and their employers, and this competition often bred corruption. The process of cruising surveyed land began with acquiring the government plats at the local land office, traveling to lands of interest, cruising the land, recording the descriptions that appealed to the cruiser, traveling back to the land office, and finally entering a claim. During the time that elapsed from the acquisition of government plats to the time when a cruiser could return to the land office to enter his claim, lands were often claimed by different cruisers working for rival employers. By 1870 Northern Wisconsin was crawling with cruisers, all looking for profitable investments for the various companies they represented. Webber and Shepard embarked on their Wisconsin River Valley cruising trip approximately the same time Anderson Brown of the Stevens Point Boomage Company cruised the area. Running into a rival cruiser while land looking always made for an anxious moment. Both parties knew they intended to claim much of the same area. This situation often resulted in a "race" back to the land office. Losing this race rendered the entire cruising trip fruitless. The winner, assuming the land was not claimed by a third party in his absence, counted himself very fortunate.[20]

---

[19] Warren, The Pioneer Woodsman, 22-25; Nesbit, Wisconsin: A History, 138; Olsen, Birth of a City, 28.

[20] Warren, The Pioneer Woodsman, 26-27, 49-54; Olsen, Birth of a City, 27, 64-65. Warren gives a vivid account of this situation through his own experience while cruising timber near Pelican Rapids. See pages: 49-54. Olsen recounts Anderson Brown's frustration in dealing with this situation. See pages: 64-65. Additionally, this competitive nature resulted in a serious problem of corrupted government officials who manned the land offices. In fact the land office at Eau Claire, under the corrupt charge of H.C. Putnum, was forced to close due to widespread corruption in 1872.

The competitive nature of the land business induced speculators and lumber companies to seek out the most accurate and honest cruisers available. Timber cruisers lived and died by their reputations, and E.S. Shepard acquired one of the best in the trade. In 1881 Shepard was listed among the leading citizens of New London in *The History of Northern Wisconsin*. The publication spoke highly of Shepard's cruising ability, stating that he "has carved out a very comfortable position in the world; beginning at fourteen years of age, he has thoroughly mastered his business, and knows Northern Wisconsin like a book..." Four years later, Rhinelander's *New North* described Shepard as "one of the best posted woodsmen" and as "thoroughly conversant with the northern country." By 1892 Shepard was penning articles describing Northern Minnesota's natural resources for an industry trade journal, *Northwestern Lumberman*, and St. Paul-Minneapolis newspapers. His word had become respected throughout the region and the *New North* proudly boasted: "If anybody thinks that Shepard won't start people talking about any country he becomes identified with they are simply off, that's all." Some fifty years after his death, one historian concisely summed up Shepard's cruising career: "From earliest manhood on, he was ranked as one of the top five timber cruisers in the country."[21]

The reputations of timber cruisers directly defined their employment options, of which there were three

---

See: Olsen, Birth of a City, 49-54; Warren, The Pioneer Woodsman, 44-45; Gates, The Wisconsin Pine Lands of Cornell University, 114-20.

[21] New North, May 28, 1885, p. 1, and December 24, 1885, p. 1; Eugene S. Shepard, "The New Northern Country," Northwestern Lumberman (January, 23, 1892), p.1; New North, January 28, 1892, p. 5; "Hoax Alive and Well: Hodag Fooled Some People for a Time," Wisconsin Then and Now, 22:1, August 1975, p. 3.

general categories: government work; working in the employ, as a payrolled employee, of land speculators or lumber companies; and working by the job as a subcontractor. Government work primarily involved the execution of the government surveys, but appointments as county surveyors, receiving contracts to produce maps, and being hired to plat road routes were also possibilities. Most government employees eventually became private timber cruisers or worked in both capacities at the same time. Working in the employ of large lumber companies was very common. Companies developed their own cruising departments and often employed large numbers of cruisers. Working as a subcontractor meant becoming a land agent or a real estate broker. This last category required a extraordinary reputation as competition was fierce, and only a fraction of lumber companies did not possess their own crews. Eugene Shepard, at different points in his career, worked in all three of the above capacities.[22]

After a short apprenticeship with A.A. Webber, Shepard found employment with absentee land speculators and local lumber companies. From the mid 1870s through the early 1880s, Shepard surveyed and brokered land for Cornell University, the largest and most successful investor in Wisconsin pine lands. He also cruised for the lumber companies that began to buy tracts, or "stumpage rights," from speculators like Cornell or the government. In this capacity he found employment with the Weyerhauser Syndicate and the Goodyear Company. In fact, Goodyear continually contracted Shepard over a span of 35 years, and he became a close friend of the family. In addition to these endeavors, Shepard also found employment with numerous other speculators and lumbering firms. By 1881, he had cultivated "a large business, locating lands, estimating

---

[22] Ryan, "The Forgotten Cruiser," 30; Ryan, "The Timber Cruiser," 27; Nesbit, Wisconsin: A History, 142.

values of timbers and lands, and preventing timber steals from lands in his charge." The following year, Shepard moved his business to the newly founded lumbering hamlet of Rhinelander and established the Northwestern Land Agency. Although he continued to reside in New London until 1886, he maintained an office in Rhinelander which became his new cruising headquarters.[23]

Shepard, through the Northwestern Land Agency, performed a host of activities while using the skills he acquired as a timber cruiser. His company, like most agencies, provided map-making services and acted as a broker for land transfers. Shepard located tracts of land and entered land transactions at the local land offices for his employers. He also protected lands from timber-thieving lumber companies. This service required Shepard to continually inspect his employer's parcels and report any illegal cutting of timber. Shepard and other land agents also paid taxes for absentee land speculators. In Wisconsin property taxes were to be paid at the county seats instead of the state capital; this requirement made it extremely difficult for absentee land speculators to pay their various taxes without employing local agents. Much of Shepard's business, however, came in contracts acquired from the local government. These contracts required Shepard to produce city, county and regional maps; plat lots throughout the city; cruise state park lands; and plat road routes. Significantly, one of these contracts required Shepard to plat the "Minneapolis road," which connected

---

[23] "Hoax Alive and Well," 3; Andreas, History of Northern Wisconsin, 1095; New North, December 14, 1882, pp.1, 4; Even into the last years of Shepard's life he maintained a close relationship to the Goodyear Company and an intimate friendship with the Goodyear family. In a letter to Mr. Nuzum, dated 12-22-1922, Shepard's affections can be seen. The letter shows that he bitterly resents a man, whom he refers to as a "downright crook" for stealing from the company.

Rhinelander to the Minnesota city.[24]

The many real estate companies and land agencies that sprang up in Rhinelander during the city's founding years emphasize the profitability of the land trade. In addition to the Northwestern Land Agency, D.E. Briggs-- Land Agent, Baily and Rife's Northern Wisconsin Land Agency, Chafee & Brown Real Estate, Insurance and Collection Agency, and Sievwright & Barnes Real Estate Agents all advertised frequently in the *New North*. All of these companies offered the same services: surveying, brokering, estimating, collecting trespassers, and attending to the payment of taxes. Additionally, the advertisements of these agencies illustrated the changing market of the land agency trade. Originally the companies marketed only pine to speculators and lumber companies. As much of the land around Rhinelander was logged off, however, the companies began to solicit the homesteader as well as absentee speculators and lumber companies. Advertisements soon included references to hardwoods to supplement the declining stands of pine. Finally, during the early twentieth century, the land agencies began to cater to potential farmers. A comparison of two of Shepard's advertisements from 1882 and 1885 and a reproduction of his company's letterhead used during the first two decades of the twentieth century illustrate this trend (see figures 1.3-1.5).[25]

---

[24] New North, March 4, 1886, p.1, March 25, 1886, p.1, May 6, 1886, p.1, January 6, 1887, p.1, April 14, 1892, p.5, August 5, 1897, p.1, and September 16, 1897, p.1. For a discussion of duties of timber cruisers see: Gates, The Wisconsin Pine Lands of Cornell University, 70-71, 87-88, 92, 200, 236.

[25] New North, December 14, 1882, p.4, August 9, 1883, p.1, June 17, 1886, p.1, and June 30, 1887, p.1.

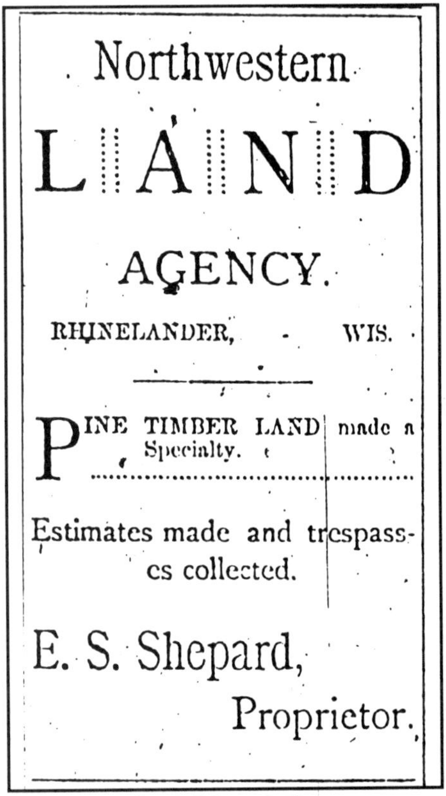

Figure 1.3: This ad first appeared in the *New North* in December, 1882. It targets lumber companies solely.

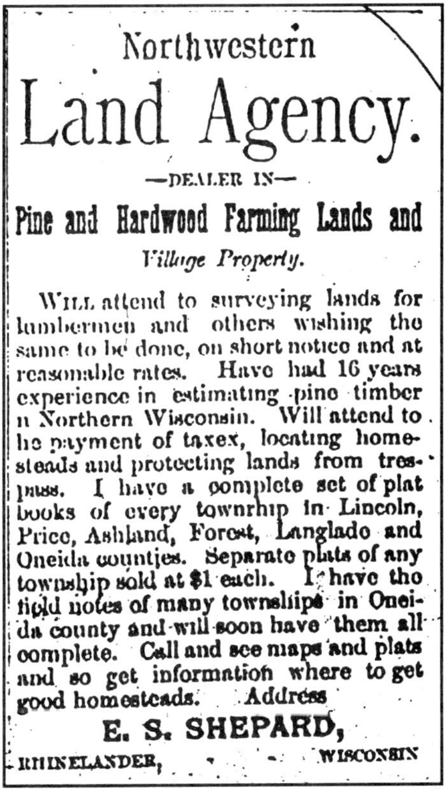

Northwestern

Land Agency.

—DEALER IN—

Pine and Hardwood Farming Lands and

Village Property.

WILL attend to surveying lands for lumbermen and others wishing the same to be done, on short notice and at reasonable rates. Have had 16 years experience in estimating pine timber n Northern Wisconsin. Will attend to the payment of taxex, locating homesteads and protecting lands from trespass. I have a complete set of plat books of every township in Lincoln, Price, Ashland, Forest, Langlade and Oneida counties. Separate plats of any township sold at $1 each. I have the field notes of many townships in Oneida county and will soon have them all complete. Call and see maps and plats and so get information where to get good homesteads. Address

E. S. SHEPARD,

RHINELANDER, WISCONSIN

Figure 1.4: This ad first appeared in the *New North* in December, 1885. It targets homesteaders and farmers in addition to lumber companies.

1 Den
2 Barn
3 House

"The Pines" Rhinelander Wis., July 3 1917
E.S. Shepard dealer in timber and farm lands

Figure 1.5: This letterhead's caption illustrates that Shepard, by the first decades of the 20th century, began to cater to prospective farmers.

Most timber cruisers who became self-employed as land agents began to speculate on their own account in addition to serving as agents for absentee speculators and lumber companies. The concept of the business remained constant for both resident and absentee speculators: purchase land at a low rate, hold on to the investment until an increase in demand raised the value of the land, and sell it on a favorable market. The resident speculators, however, invested on a much smaller scale and were usually unable to hold their investment for an extended period, since taxes soon exhausted their resources. Additionally, resident speculators were treated differently by local settlers. Absentee speculators were viewed as exploiters of the resources, hindering settlement by holding on to the choicest lands and paying taxes in only the most lethargic manner. Worst of all, absentee speculators were seen as stealing the financial benefits of the locality to invest elsewhere. Local speculators, by contrast, were usually prominent local citizens concerned about the growth and prosperity of the community. These speculators had a stake in the advancement of the region, paid taxes promptly, and, most importantly, reinvested their wealth in the community.[26]

E.S. Shepard, in various instances from the 1880s onward, acted as a resident land speculator. His most extensive venture took place from 1891 through 1895. During this period Shepard split his time equally between Rhinelander and the Rainy River Valley which defines the Minnesota and Ontario, Canada border. During the summer of 1891 Shepard embarked on an extended land-looking venture to Rainy River and as far northwest as Lake of the Woods. Shepard was impressed with the country and intrigued by the opportunities it possessed. Understating his excitement he concluded that the country "was good enough for us." It was so good, in fact, that

---

[26] Gates, The Wisconsin Pine Lands of Cornell University, 68.

Shepard purchased a large tract of land from the federal government on the Rainy River. In November of 1891 he returned to the area with his mentor and cruising partner, A.A. Webber. The two men arrived at a location on the Rainy River about twenty-two miles by water west of present day International Falls, Minnesota. This location marks the confluence of the Rainy and Big Fork Rivers. They arrived "on the 9th day of November, [1891] and named the spot Hannaford after the Northern Pacific Ry. Traffic Manager." The two men erected a block cabin in time to entertain the "American subjects in the valley" by hosting a Thanksgiving Day dinner.[27]

During 1892 and 1893 Shepard returned often to his "new town," as the *New North* dubbed Hannaford. In April of 1892 Shepard returned to the region with Tim Conners of Merrill, Wisconsin, who contemplated erecting a hotel at the site. In the Spring of 1894, Shepard, along with a crew of four, returned to the location "to plat the village of Hannaford on Rainy river [*sic*]." The region was only recently opened for settlement by the federal government, and Shepard assured himself that Hannaford would soon experience a boom. On their return he explained "we met many teams and men rushing for the new Rainy River district, Hannaford and Rainy Lake City.... Now that the country is open it will settle fast." That same year the optimistic timber cruiser established the Hannaford Improvement Company, and he reported that the town had indeed begun to flourish.[28] As early as 1891 it looked probable that Shepard would leave Rhinelander for Hannaford permanently, and the *New North* sadly reflected:

---

[27] Eugene Shepard, "To the Rainy River," New North, August 13, 1891, p.1; Shepard, "The Big Fork Country," New North, December 17, 1891, p.1.

[28] Eugene Shepard, "A trip to Hannaford," New North, March 22, 1894, p.1; New North, March 22, 1894, p.1.

It is quite likely that [Shepard] will go [to Hannaford] permanently. Mr Shepard has lived in Rhinelander since its first start, and many of the improvements which have taken place since ...are in quite a measure due to his efforts. His many friends here will wish him unbounded success wherever he may locate.[29]

In 1893, however, depression struck the country, and in August of 1894 Shepard admitted "that the condition of business everywhere has affected even the new country in Northern Minnesota, but that [Hannaford] will boom when business finally picks up." Business never picked up to the pace Shepard had envisioned, and his dream of creating a thriving city slowly faded. By 1896, he had lost interest in his fluttering project and the expense of property tax most likely forced Shepard to liquidate his investment. Today the confluence of the Rainy and Big Fork Rivers does not bear the name of Hannaford, nor is the location even denoted as a town. Shepard's letter to the *New North* describing repeated trips to "his city," were perhaps the best result of the whole affair. These letters describe in detail the trips and their various routes, and they represent first-hand accounts of the area as it was in the 1890s. In addition, much of Shepard's personality and humor is readily apparent.[30]

After the turn of the century, Shepard continued to act as an agent of lumber companies, and he made numerous purchases for various firms. For example, he purchased 6400 acres in Minnesota for the Goodyear Company in early April, 1905. In addition to these activities, however, he continued to act as his own agent,

[29] New North, October 15, 1891, p.5.

[30] Ibid., August 9, 1894, p.1. For Shepard's letters, see: "To Rainy River," New North, August 13, 1891, p.1; "Big Fork Country," New North, December 17, 1891, p.1; "A Trip to Hannaford," New North, March 22, 1894.

purchasing timber tracts comprised mostly of hardwoods or small stands of previously overlooked pine. He marketed these lands and sold them to lumbering and milling firms. In late November of 1905, Shepard entered into one of these investments, purchasing 47,000 acres north of Rhinelander. The tract contained "480,000,000 of standing timber consisting of pine, hemlock, birch, basswood and other hardwood timber." Shepard announced in a short *New North* article that the timber contained on the tract could be processed by the milling firms in Rhinelander. Speaking to the saw mills the article concluded: "Substitutes for the pine that has faded away must be taken in; there is no excuse for going west or south and entering new fields while supplies are within reach of their plants and market." Simultaneously, Shepard began to invest in the cut-over lands of Oneida County. By purchasing large tracts of stumps, sectioning the land into homesteads, and marketing it as agricultural lands, Shepard, like many other entrepreneurs in Northern Wisconsin, began to exploit lands discarded by the lumber trade. In just one example from early April of 1903, Shepard brought a group of settlers to Oneida County from Iowa and Minnesota who purchased and improved 1000 acres of his cut-over lands for the purpose of farming.[31]

Eugene Shepard worked as a timber cruiser, served as an agent of absentee speculators, and engaged in land speculation on his own account. These activities proved extremely profitable for Shepard and he became one of Rhinelander's wealthiest citizens. Timber cruisers were paid by the amount of land they reported on, or by the number of days they were engaged in cruising for their employers. Henry C. Putnam, the local agent Ezra Cornell employed in Wisconsin, compensated timber cruisers at "$10 for each quarter section which they reported to have

---

[31] *New North*, April 6, 1905, p.1, November 23, 1905, p.1, and April 2, 1903, p.1.

pine in commercial quantities and to be close to rivers suitable for floating logs to mills." In addition, Putnam often paid for the expenses of his cruisers. At this rate of pay, the cruisers found it unprofitable to evaluate the pine stands in great detail and they reported only the general characteristics of the parcels they recommended. As a result, much of the land purchased by Cornell had to be reevaluated in greater detail at a later date. Shepard, for more detailed cruising assignments, was compensated at "$4 to $5 per day plus expenses." Although a cruiser's compensation seems trivial compared to the financial gain their employers reaped, they were paid much better then their counterparts working in the lumber camps and saw mills.[32]

As Shepard began to serve as a local agent for absentee speculators his earning potential rose substantially. Agents were compensated for evaluating and selecting lands, entering lands at the local land offices, and managing the investments of their employers. This last service included paying taxes promptly, protecting pine stands from timber thieves and brokering the land when it came time to sell. For selecting and entering tracts of pine, Wisconsin agents were often compensated in parcels of land. The usual practice deeded one quarter of the total land entered to the local agent. It was also common, however, for speculators to pay their agents in currency. This second form of compensation was most often used

---

[32] Gates, The Wisconsin Pine Lands of Cornell University, 103; Eugene Shepard vs Mildred Shepard, "Finding of Fact," Oneida County Circuit Court--Civil, Box #30, Volume #3, Case #1302, Filed September 22, 1909. Theoretically, cruisers employed under the terms Putnam provided could report bogus parcels of usable pine and receive compensation. However, their employers would eventually discover the deception, and immediately ruin the reputation of less-then-honest cruisers. The important role the cruiser's reputation played in procuring employment kept them honest.

when local agents selected farmlands for speculators. According to Paul Gates: "The price [paid to agents] for entering farming land ranged from $15 to $25 a quarter section. Some agents selected and entered land for $10 a quarter section, but...they did nothing further in the way of managing the land." In addition to charging a higher rate for lands they entered, agents that maintained the investments of their employers also received compensation for specific services. For example, speculators usually paid their agents a small percentage, normally around five percent, of the taxes the latter paid for them. Finally, local agents played a crucial role in the transfer of land owned by absentee speculators to lumber companies or other buyers. In such instances, agents were compensated on a commission basis. Being paid a percentage of large land transactions proved to be a profitable engagement. Chroniclers of Shepard's hoaxes report that Shepard made several fortunes cruising timber. In 1905, an unsubstantiated but often quoted story tells us, he netted over $50,000 after an extended cruising trip in California.[33] The $50,000 Shepard allegedly earned, was undoubtedly a

---

[33] This profitable cruising trip to California is often quoted by local historians and professional writers as occurring in 1903. These accounts go on to state that Shepard used his earnings to purchase an elaborate residence he entitled "The Pines." In January of 1906 Shepard purchased "the Pines," two expensive race horses, invested in several pieces of Rhinelander real estate, and took his wife and youngest son on a three-month tour of California. This activity suggests that Shepard had realized an enormous financial gain through his cruising activities. I have discovered no record, save hear-say, as to the amount of money Shepard was paid for his services in California. See: New North, May 3, 1906, p.6, and May 17, 1906, p.5; Vindicator (Rhinelander, Wisconsin) January 3, 1906, p.5, January 3, 1906, p.4, and January 10, 1906, p.5; Rhinelander Herald (Rhinelander, Wisconsin) February 10, 1906, p.5.

commission paid him for brokering a large deal.[34]

As local agents made large sums of money and received lands from their services, they often began to speculate on their own account. This, of course, offered an even greater promise of financial gain. Depending on the market and the state of the economy, agents could profit enormously from well-advised speculation. This enterprise, however, carried a great risk. The down side of speculation is clearly seen in Shepard's failed speculation endeavors on the Rainy River. Overall, Shepard did well financially in all of his roles in the land business. In a 1909 evaluation of Shepard's past income potential, the Oneida County Civil Court concluded that he had "speculated in timber and wild lands and dealt in them as a commission broker and at times has made large gains in income."[35]

In addition to the financial promise of the cruising and speculating trade, it is clear that other factors encouraged men to cruise the woods. Although few cruisers wrote of their experiences, those who did often reflected on other benefits of their employment besides compensation. The letters that Shepard penned from his trips to the northern boundary of Minnesota included many of these themes. The same themes are present in George Warren's *The Pioneer Woodsman as He is Related to Lumbering in the Northwest*, a first hand account of a timber cruiser working in the same area and period as Shepard. The identification with the Ojibwa Indians (a tribe of Northern Wisconsin and Minnesota) and the cruisers' reverence for the land are perhaps the most interesting of these common themes.

---

[34] Gates, The Wisconsin Pine Lands of Cornell University, 92, 81.

[35] Eugene Shepard vs Mildred Shepard, "Findings of Fact," Case #1302.

Cruisers depended on Native Americans for occasional assistance, food, and shelter. They developed an understanding of, if not respect for, Native American cultures. Although Warren expresses this better than Shepard did in his letters, Shepard later created an elaborate exhibit for the Oneida County Fair explaining and honoring the Ojibwa Culture. Additionally, Shepard's relationship with the Ojibwa was mentioned at the end of his life in a *New North* obituary: "Among the Indians he was well known, especially among the tribesmen who inhabit this part of the state, chiefly the Chippewas. He knew well their customs, and could speak their language."[36] Both Warren and Shepard were fluent in the Ojibwa languages and folkways, and each man took advantage of the tribe's hospitality and hired tribal members as assistants.

In addition, cruisers often became attached to the land they worked with. Although judging people's motives is a difficult and dangerous task, it is safe to say that a love of the trade, nature and the woods played an important role in inducing these men to return to the woods time after time. Warren explained:

> There is doubt whether or not anything finer enters into the joy of living than being in the solitude of the great unbroken forest, surrounded by magnificent, tall, straight, beautiful pine trees, on a day when the sun is casting shadows through their waving tops, listening to the whisperings, form almost into words, of the needle-like fingers of their leafy boughs, to the warbling of the songsters, and to the chirping of the almost saucy, yet sociable red squirrel who is sure to let one know that he has invaded his dominion. Such days, with such scenes and emotions, do come in the life of a woodsman, the land hunter, who is alone in the forest, except that if he be at all sentimental, he approaches nearer to the Great Creator than

---

[36] "Life Closes For Eugene Shepard," New North, March 29, 1923, p.1.

almost any time in his life's experiences.[37]

Shepard's expression of this feeling of reverence to the land and closeness to nature sounds remarkably similar to his counterpart's. Interestingly, Shepard, like Warren, utilized religious connotations in describing the effect of the woods:

> I have learned to love the woods and all that belong to them.... All the places I've just mentioned [Minnesota, Michigan, Canada and the West Coast] have their beautiful spots but give me northern Wisconsin for my permanent tramping ground! It's a glimpse of heaven to see the tall pine trees, with their candle like tips; the myriad lakes, with water clear and crystal; the streams, bordered with pine, spruce and balsam, with here and there the white bark of the birch! ...it seemed too bad that of all the people in and around northern Wisconsin, only a few cruisers should enjoy all this wild and natural beauty...[38]

After the lumber industry proliferated in the Middle West and before technology and the emergence of university-educated foresters pushed the woodsman from the trade, the forests were filled with old-style cruisers like Shepard. These men provided a needed skill and developed a deeply felt love for the woods. Several men, like Eugene Shepard, adopted the skills they acquired as timber cruisers and became land agents and resident land speculators. Although resident land speculation did not

---

[37] Warren, The Pioneer Woodsman, 48-49.

[38] Eugene S. and Karretta Gunderson Shepard, Paul Bunyan His Camp and His Wife (Tomahawk, Wisconsin, 1929), 11. This description of the natural beauty of the woods was part of E.S. Shepard's explanation of why he created the hodag (so that others might come to Rhinelander, in search of the hodag, and witness the beauty of the area first hand). The book, a compilation of Shepard's short stories of Bunyan and other lumberjack lore, was published six years after his death by his second wife Karretta Gunderson Shepard.

share the enormous potential absentee speculation did, it was, nevertheless, a profitable business. Ironically, the cruisers, local land agents and resident land speculators were agents of an industry that altered beyond recognition, if not destroyed completely, the very thing that brought them such joy and satisfaction.

CHAPTER II

EUGENE SHEPARD AND RHINELANDER, WI.

An 1898 estimate concluded that the upper nineteen counties of Wisconsin, the state's northern pineries, contained 129,400,000,000 board feet of lumber. The extent of this resource and the mid nineteenth-century developing need for timber in the recently opened prairie lands west of Wisconsin, dictated the settlement and history of the region. As a result, the northern cities within the Wisconsin River Valley shared a common history. Stevens Point, Wausau, Mosinee, Merrill and Rhinelander were all founded and initially developed by the lumber industry.[1]

The timber lands of the upper Wisconsin were not purchased during the opening auction in 1866 because of concerns over the river's ability to economically transport logs to markets farther south. The northern portion of the Wisconsin River moves rapidly, has sharp directional changes, endures rapids and falls, and is dotted with numerous islands. Furthermore, the river is extremely shallow in its northern sections and its shifting bottom creates an additional hazard of moving sandbars. All of

---

[1] Robert C. Nesbit, Urbanization and Industrialization, 1873-1893, vol. 3, The History of Wisconsin (Madison, 1985), 46-48; Kurt Kortenhof, Sugar Camp 1891-1941: The Origin and Early History of a Northern Wisconsin Community (Eau Claire, Wisconsin, 1993), 15; Olsen, Birth of a City, 37, 41.

these factors make the Wisconsin susceptible to log jams and, consequently, a dangerous and expensive transportation route for timber. Although the area around Pelican Rapids was, from the 1860s on, cruised continually by men employed by interested speculators and lumber companies, the difficulties posed by the river effectively dissuaded companies from purchasing the land.[2]

In 1871 Anderson Brown and Anson P. Vaughn, cruising for the E.D. Brown's Stevens Point Boomage Company, inspected the pine stands around Pelican Rapids. The natural advantages of Pelican Rapids made it an ideal location for a lumbering enterprise. Approximately "one and one half billions of standing pine within a twenty mile circle" surrounded the rapids. The rapids fell 22 feet in 100 rods and had the potential to power sawmills. In addition, low swampland around what was then called "Fish Lake" by local Ojibwas, offered an easily flooded area which could create a holding area or "logging boom." The two cruisers enthusiastically reported their findings to E.D. Brown upon their return to Stevens Point. Despite the natural advantages Pelican Rapids offered, E.D. Brown was reluctant to enter into the venture. The problems the Wisconsin River caused for lumbering weighed heavy in the decision. The Browns had to wait for the extension of rail trackage, then just beginning to emerge, to ensure the profitability of a venture at Pelican Rapids. The difficulties posed by the Wisconsin River postponed the founding of Rhinelander for over a decade.[3]

In 1878 E.D. Brown was finally convinced to take a chance at Pelican Rapids. In that year the Brown family

---

[2] August Derleth, The Wisconsin: River of a Thousand Isles (New York, 1942), 174-76; Olsen, Birth of a City, 28, 32.

[3] Ibid., 28-31, 38, 41; George O. Jones, et al., History of Lincoln, Oneida, and Vilas Counties (Minneapolis and Winona, Minnesota, 1924), 114. The low swampland around Fish Lake would eventually be flooded and present-day Boom Lake created.

purchased 1500 acres of land from the federal government at the location. The family sat on their investment for four years until they convinced the Milwaukee, Lake Shore, and Western Railroad (later this railroad became part of the Chicago and Northwestern Railroad) to run through Rhinelander en route to Lake Superior. In return for half of the Brown family's holdings at Pelican Rapids, the railroad agreed to connect the location with its network of track. In 1882 the extension was completed, a city platted and named Rhinelander honoring the president of the railroad.[4]

Between 1871 and 1882 Andy Brown returned to Pelican Rapids numerous times. On many of these trips he ran into Eugene Shepard, who was constantly engaged in cruising tracts of land in the same vicinity. The two became acquainted and developed a friendship that lasted a lifetime. Shepard recalled years later that he "had met Mr. Anderson Brown on exploring trips up river and on the stages coming back and forth." Knowing the natural advantages of the area, the competence of the Brown family, and the importance of a rail connection, Shepard understood the opportunities available in 1882:

> The Milwaukee Lake Shore & Western Railway was pushing north for somewhere on Lake Superior so one day I was at the [Wausau] Land Office, I found a goodly chunk of land had been purchased by that Stevens Point family of Browns and A.T. Anderson, an uncle of theirs.... The Ry. Co. built a line into the place in the fall of 1882, and I made up my mind to be there also on the ground floor.[5]

Despite the relatively late founding of Rhinelander, settlement proceeded in a hurry. By November of 1882,

---

[4] Kortenhof, Sugar Camp, 18.

[5] Olsen, The Birth of a City, 35-36; Shepard, "Reminiscences," New North December 12, 1912.

lumberjacks, hoping to find employment in the woods that
winter, flocked to the new city before the railroad even
completed its extension.   Shepard's own account of
Rhinelander's first days reveals that the city was nothing
more than a handful of tents. One of these tents was quite
large and acted as the hamlet's first hotel, but it was
constantly overcrowded and men slept on the floor.
Eugene Shepard spent his first night in Rhinelander
sleeping on the floor of this tent-hotel. Shepard recalled
that the town "grew like magic" as many of the "downriver
lumbermen made [it] their headquarters." Two years after
its founding, Rhinelander boasted a population of 1,500
inhabitants. By 1891, the city served as the headquarters
of over 40 lumbering firms and housed eight sawmills.[6]

Although Shepard did not move his residence to
Rhinelander during 1882, he spent the fall and winter in the
new boomtown. His wife and son remained in New
London, as did his permanent address, while Shepard
established his Northwestern Land Agency in Rhinelander.
His office, located in what was known as "Shepard's land
office block," was under construction when the second
issue of the *New North* was published on December 14,
1882. The building was completed early the following
March, and Shepard began renting office space to other
entrepreneurs. Shepard rented space to, among others, the

[6] Ibid., December 12, 1912; New North, December 1, 1893,
p.1; Kortenhof, Sugar Camp, 17. For general works on the history
of Rhinelander see: Jones, George O., Norman S. Mcvean, et al.
History of Lincoln, Oneida, and Vilas Counties (Minneapolis and
Winona, Minnesota, 1924), 113-19; T.V. Olsen, Our First Hundred
Years: A History of Rhinelander (Rhinelander, 1981); T.V. Olsen,
Birth of a City: The Rhinelander Country, Volume Two
(Rhinelander, 1983); Alman I. Lord, Industrial Review of
Rhinelander, Wis. (Rhinelander, 1898); Harvey Huston, '93/'43
Thunder Lake Narrow Gauge (Winnetka, Illinois), 1963. See also
the following: the thirtieth anniversary issue of the New North
December 12, 1912; "Rhinelander," (in six parts) New North,
December 1, 1892 through January 19, 1893.

architect and builder A.M. Melcher (who constructed the building) and to Rhinelander's first lawyer, G.H. Peters.[7]

In addition to his land office, Shepard put together a logging crew and operated a lumber camp just three miles from the city throughout the winter of 1882 and 1883. This appears to be one of the only times Shepard endeavored to harvest timber on his own account. Although the lumbering industry offered vast opportunities, not all who entered the trade turned a profit.   In Rhinelander, as elsewhere during this period, the small operations were often pushed out of the business. Shepard's lumbering endeavor became one of these unsuccessful ventures.   Whether Shepard's lumber camp made or lost money in the winter of 1882 and 1883 is unknown. Regardless, it is clear that Shepard realized that his true abilities lay in speculating the resource, not harvesting it.   Shepard's camp broke up in early March because of deep snow. His camp was the first in the area to break up. The next winter, as the lumber camps were again established throughout the northwoods, Shepard's was not among them.[8]

After March of 1883, Shepard spent much less time in Rhinelander, and advertisements for his land agency disappeared in August of that year. It is unclear whether he continued to operate his business from Rhinelander or

---

[7] New North, December 14, 1882, p.1, and March 22, 1883, p.1; Olsen, Our First Hundred Years, 22, 52. According to Olsen the first issues of the New North were printed in a makeshift office located in a tent. This helps affirm Shepard's account of the rapid pace at which Rhinelander emerged.

[8] New North, January 11, 1883, p.1, and March 1, 1883, p.1; Olsen, The Birth of a City, 136. During the Autumn of 1890 Shepard announced plans to harvest 4000 cords of poplar pulp timber eight miles east of Rhinelander. It is unclear if his plans to harvest the timber ever materialized. See: Vindicator, November 19, 1890, p.5.

his home in New London for the next two years. It is
clear, however, that he frequented Rhinelander. Often
staying as long as a week in Rhinelander's premier hotel,
the Rapids House, Shepard was constantly "looking over'
the town" during 1883 and 1884. The editor of the *New
North*, familiar with Shepard and realizing that his
reputation and ingenuity would be a great advantage for the
budding city, kept close tabs on the popular land agent.
With a sense of pride and excitement the *New North*
announced in the summer of 1885 that "E.S. Shepard, the
New London pine land man is looking after interests in this
vicinity. It is understood Mr. S[hepard] intends to move
his family to Rhinelander this summer and thereafter make
his home here."[9]

Although Shepard did not relocate to Rhinelander in
the summer of 1885 as the *New North* had hopefully
reported, advertisements for the Northwestern Land
Agency did reappear in December of that year. Early the
following February Shepard finally made the move to
Rhinelander, although his wife Mildred and son Claude
remained in New London. On February second, the *New
North* exclaimed that "E.S. Shepard came up from New
London last week and will hereafter make Rhinelander his
headquarters. E.S. is a rusher and will do good work
toward helping Rhinelander boom, as it surely must and
will do." Shepard immediately began to build a home on
Pelham Street upon his return. By the end of April his
brother, E.A. Shepard, was plastering the inside as it
neared completion. In mid-June Shepard moved his family

---

[9] New North, August 16, 1883, p.1, and May 28, 1885, p.1.
It seems probable that Shepard sold his land agency building some
time during the spring of 1883. The New North, while reporting
Shepard's return to Rhinelander in its February 11, 1886 issue,
reported that Shepard "located his office the first door east of the
Post Office." This suggests that it was in a different location from
the original site established in the fall of 1882.

up from New London and into their new home.[10]

Upon his permanent relocation to Rhinelander Shepard quickly acquired appointments from the local government, and he played a role in the city's development as an officer of the county. His surveying expertise led to an appointment as Deputy Surveyor of Lincoln County in September of 1886. In December of 1886 the city of Rhinelander, originally part of Lincoln County, was about to become the seat of government for Oneida County (a new county to be established on January 1, 1887). In late December, the county board appointed Shepard county surveyor, a position commencing on the first day of 1887 as Oneida County came into being. Shepard conducted his duties as a county surveyor, which included surveying and platting government lands and assisting in government land sales and transfers, while continuing to run his private land agency. In early February, his role as county surveyor took him to the State Land Office in Madison to look after the concerns of the new county.[11]

The following spring, Shepard and 29 others were appointed Special Land Surveyors for Oneida County. These temporary appointments fulfilled the requirements of section 1053 of the 1878 revised state statutes which required "the securing of the correct valuation of the property of Oneida County." The appointments were made on March 16th, 1887, and the work was to be completed by June 20th of the same year. Each inspector received a generous compensation of $6.00 per day, and each

---

[10] New North, February 4, 1886, p.1, April 22, 1886, p.1, April 29, 1886, p.1, and June 17, 1886, p.1.

[11] Ibid., September 23, 1886, p.1, December 23, 1886, p.1, and February 10, 1887, p.1. This practice of establishing new counties in northern Wisconsin, including Oneida from Lincoln, was one of conflict and corruption. For a good description see: Gates, The Wisconsin Pine Lands of Cornell University, 145-151.

employed two assistants at $4.00 per day.[12]

The week following these appointments a long letter printed on the front page of the *New North* questioned the county board's appointment of the special inspectors. The letter, signed "A Taxpayer," questioned the legitimacy of the appointments and raised some interesting questions. The author of the protest estimated that it would cost the county $35,280 to evaluate the 2100 sections within the new county. The amount paid to the inspectors, the protestor insisted, was "double the price which any businessman would agree to pay" for the same service. This bill would undoubtedly be footed by the taxpayers of the county, because the county treasury had "not enough money...to pay the quarter salary of a single officer." In addition, the protest continued, the inspections would prove useless as "the motley crowd of so-called land inspectors" were unqualified.[13]

The successful move by the people of Rhinelander to create Oneida County from Lincoln was undertaken partly because many believed (probably correctly) that Lincoln County was controlled by a "ring" that unfairly taxed the county's inhabitants. Contracts were awarded which benefited, often directly, members of the board. The "taxpayer's" protest objected that the new Oneida County Board was engaging in the same shady enterprise. The letter questioned: "Are the people willing to support a ring similar to that which existed so many years in Lincoln County?" It went on to remind the readers "Our pledge and main argument to the state when we asked to be cut off from Lincoln County was that we could and would give to the tax payer a more economical management of

[12] New North, April 7, 1887, p. 4.

[13] Ibid., April 14, 1887, p.1.

county affairs."[14]

On April 18th, E.O. and A.W. Brown moved a resolution to rescind the appointment of the inspectors on the grounds that "the compensation of said inspectors will create a large indebtedness against the county and no provisions have been made for paying it." It appears that Henry W. Sage, an absentee land speculator with large holdings in Oneida County, penned the protest letter. In addition, the Brown Brothers Lumber Company held most of the locally-owned land in Oneida County. The tax burden, most likely levied as a property tax, would fall disproportionately on Sage and the Brown company holdings. Of the three board members, only A.W. Brown voted for the resolution. The other two members, W.L. Beers and T.B. Walsh, voted the measure down. The wages paid the inspectors might well have been high and some of the land inspectors (excluding Shepard, of course) may have been inexperienced. The fact remains, however, that state law required a survey to be taken. That the expense fell disproportionately on the segment of the population that gained the most from the resources of the northwoods possibly suggests that justice was done. It is clear, however, that the board allocated more money than it needed to for this project - a practice that directly or indirectly benefited its members. In any event, Shepard completed his work in September and received $165.00 for his services.[15]

During the following May, Shepard received an appointment as Register of Deeds of Oneida County by

---

[14]   Ibid., April 14, 1887, p.1.

[15]   New North, October 6, 1887, p.5; Gates, The Wisconsin Pine Lands of Cornell University, 155-56. Gates views this conflict as a single episode in a larger tradition that pitted self-serving county board tax leviers against the protests of exploiting absentee speculators. In summation, Gates stated that each side "fought corruption with corruption (161)."

Wisconsin's Governor Rust. Initially Shepard continued to act as county surveyor, but he soon found the work load too heavy. By the end of June, Shepard resigned his surveying post. Despite the subsequent appointment of C.A. Norway as deputy register of deeds, Shepard soon hired Daniel Graham, the same man who succeeded him as county surveyor, to temporarily conduct the business of the Northwestern Land Agency. Shepard found the work of his post too restricting; it often forced him to stay in the county and he was unable to cruise as he wished. In January of 1891, Shepard resigned his post as register of deeds to pursue the business of his land agency full time. Although this ended Shepard's work as a government officer of the county, it freed him to more fully pursue another activity perhaps more important to Rhinelander and Oneida County.[16]

Since Rhinelander's conception, Eugene Shepard was one of the city's most enthusiastic and successful city boosters. Boosterism, according to James B. Smith, "refers to the phenomenon of local citizens acting in concert for the purpose of promoting the growth of their city's population and/or the expansion of its wealth or capacity to produce wealth." It is a nineteenth- and twentieth-century "uniquely American" phenomenon, in which leading citizens act out of local pride and civic mindedness more often than a desire to amass immediate personal profit. Boosters organized themselves into permanent voluntary organizations for general promotion of their city, and they created *ad hoc* committees to promote a specific advancement or to solicit a particular industrialist

---

[16] New North, June 9, 1887, p.1, June 16, 1887, p.1, June 30, 1887, p.1, August 4, 1887, p.4, and September 15, 1887, p.6; Vindicator, November 5, 1890, p.3, and January 21, 1891, p.3. Graham's name replaced Shepard's in the advertisements of the Northwestern Land Agency from August 4, 1887 to September 15, 1887. I am inferring it was because of the duties required of Shepard as Register of Deeds.

to locate in the city. Civic-minded local newspapers often served as rallying vehicles for boosters, calling attention to the needs of the city and constantly reminding its readership to look to the future.[17]

Boosterism was not an isolated occurrence induced by the lumber industry of Wisconsin and the Midwest; it played a role in the development of turn-of-the-century America in every region of the country. The same components emerge in all areas: the role of leading citizens, the role of the newspapers, the importance of adequate transportation (in the nineteenth century this usually meant railroad links), and the diversification of industry. In the Midwest, boosters first induced lumber barons to locate in their towns and subsequently sought railroad links to facilitate shipping. As the pine stands were converted to cut-over lands, every lumber boomtown confronted the question of what to do next. Some simply ceased to exist and became ghost towns like Porterville near Eau Claire, and some were reduced to sparsely populated resort towns like Star Lake near Rhinelander. Other cities were able to become the seats of government for newly created counties, diversify their industrial complex and continue to thrive.[18]

Turn-of-the-century boosterism in Rhinelander focused on three related objectives: to foster an increase in the city population, to promote the sale of agricultural lands in the vicinity and to attract industry to the city. Clearly, growth and prosperity were synonymous to

---

[17] James B. Smith, "The Movements for Diversified Industry in Eau Claire, Wisconsin, 1879-1907: Boosterism and Urban Development Strategy In A Declining Lumber Town," (University of Wisconsin--Madison: unpublished Master's Thesis, 1967), 4-5, 174, 176. See also: Cronon, Nature's Metropolis, 31-41.

[18] Edward L. Ayers in his Promise of the New South: Life After Reconstruction (New York, 1992), describes this process of boosterism in the south around the turn of the century.

boosters in Rhinelander as they were to boosters elsewhere. Shepard explained this understanding as it related to Rhinelander in a 1907 newspaper article:

> It is hardly necessary to call attention to the benefits which will result from increased settlement and development of our northern counties and Oneida county in particular. It will benefit all classes of the community in the cities as well as in the country, the merchants will profit by an increased sales of commodities and can expand his business as the community develops...a greater production of stock make better markets and higher prices; more neighbors mean better roads, better schools and more agreeable conditions of social life. The taxpayer profits from development of more taxable property through decreased taxes as the taxable property increases as is proved by the comparison of our tax rates with those of thickly settled sections the latter being much lower.[19]

The first cry for organized boosting activity appeared in the pages of the *New North* in February of 1886, only one week after Shepard relocated to Rhinelander. The paper loudly suggested that Rhinelander needed a Business Men's Association to promote its natural advantages for lumber and industrial development. It pointed out that every successful city in the state greatly benefited from such organizations and made particular reference to the association in Oshkosh. The following week, the leading citizens complied and held an organizational meeting. The initial meeting, "well attended by the business community," appointed Eugene Shepard, A.W. Shelton and John Barnes to a committee to draft a constitution and by-laws. On February 17th the officers of the new association were elected: W.E. Brown, president; E.S. Shepard, vice president; John Barnes, Secretary; C.

---

[19] Shepard, "Boost Northern Wisconsin," New North, November 28, 1907, p.1,8.

Chafee, treasurer.[20]

It does not appear that the Business Men's Association made the type of impact the *New North* expected. In November of 1886 the paper printed renewed challenges to the organization, suggesting that it was "a good time for the Business Men's Association to wake up and make a stir." Shortly thereafter, a Big Rapids, Michigan lumbering firm under the direction of F.S. Robbins, L. Baird and J.P. Underwood announced plans to relocate to Rhinelander. This firm, originally established as Baird and Robbins Lumber Company, eventually became one of the largest operations in the area. In addition, it brought F.S. Robbins to the city, a man who himself became a influential city booster and leading entrepreneur. It is highly probable that Rhinelander, through its Business Men's Association, offered the lumbering firm inducements to bring it to Rhinelander. In fact, the company initially occupied the Brown Brothers boarding house until they could erect their own facilities.[21] Baird and Robbins represented direct competition to the Brown Brothers

---

[20] New North, February 4, 1886, p.1, and February 11, 1886, p.1. The fact that this call appeared immediately after Shepard returned to Rhinelander suggests that he might have been the instigator of the meeting. This seems more likely when one remembers the personal relationship Shepard had with the editor of the paper and the active role he proceeded to play in the association.

[21] New North, November 18, 1886, p.1; "Another Mill For Rhinelander," New North, November 25, 1886, p.1; Kortenhof, Sugar Camp, 61-64. Prior to this development, it appears that an *ad hoc* committee was established and E.S. Shepard was involved. The June 3rd issue of the New North stated: "Messrs W.H. Bradley, of Milwaukee, C.F. Fricke of Madison, accompanied E.S. Shepard to Rainbow Rapids Tuesday to examine the completed work of the Rhinelander Improvement and Transportation Company. Of this company the New North has, by request, refrained from giving details of its plans but hopes to present an extended article soon." I found no other mention of this company.

Lumber Company, but the latter took great pains to induce the former to relocate to Rhinelander (A.W. Brown, the president of the B.M.A., was one of the "Brown Brothers"). This suggests that direct personal profit was' not the motive for the actions of Rhinelander boosters. In addition, the two companies developed a friendly relationship, and several years later Robbins' narrow gauge railroad serviced Brown Brother lumber camps. In the end, the prosperity Robbins brought to Rhinelander outweighed other considerations. Only weeks after the new company began to erect its mill, the *New North* announced that 100 Michigan families sought dwellings in Rhinelander.[22]

Shepard, through his constant travels, had the opportunity to "sell Rhinelander" everywhere he went. Furthermore, his connections with major lumbering firms gave him direct access to Rhinelander's most coveted industry. In the summer of 1887, for example, he met with Michigan businessmen who were considering Rhinelander as a paper milling point. A written form of Shepard's sale pitch appeared in the columns of the *Northwestern Lumberman* shortly afterward. Shepard gave a "glowing picture of Rhinelander as a lumber manufacturers' paradise." He explained the natural advantages of the city and detailed the value of its rail connections. Finally, he declared that "he was prepared to offer big inducements to any mill firm who may desire to remove its plant to Rhinelander." The millers from Michigan were interested enough to tour Rhinelander, but they failed to relocate. The city did not, at this early point, acquire a paper mill - despite Shepard's efforts on

---

[22] New North, February 24, 1887, p.1; Kortenhof, Sugar Camp, 15-28. James Smith found the same type of cooperation in Eau Claire, suggesting booster motives other than direct personal gain were at play. See also: Huston, Thunder Lake Narrow Gauge.

behalf of the B.M.A.[23]

Despite the failure to attract a paper mill, Rhinelander expanded rapidly in 1887. The population and valuation of the city doubled within the year, and a second railroad, the Soo Line, connected Rhinelander to its network of lines in the last months of 1886.[24] The lumber industry boomed and the *New North* published a favorable assessment of the year's achievements in December. Even at this point, however, there appears to have been an uneasy feeling among the city leaders. They knew that the pine stands were rapidly depleting and that Rhinelander needed to look to a future beyond the disappearing pine. At the end of November, 1887, Shepard called a meeting of the B.M.A. to discuss strategies for attracting other industry in addition to that of lumbering. Only five years after its founding, Rhinelander had begun its attempt to diversify.[25]

---

[23] Northwestern Lumberman 30, no. 6, (August 6, 1887), p.6; "Gene and the Chicagoans," New North, August 11, 1887, p.1.

[24] The process in which the Soo Line was induced to run through Rhinelander is an interesting example of community boosterism in itself. Initially the line had planned to bypass Rhinelander, but the Brown Brothers Lumber Company "gave one third of the land they possessed" to the railroad. Likewise, the Milwaukee, Lake Shore & Western Railroad, already connected with Rhinelander, offered a similar bonus. After the Soo Line accepted the offer, the two railroad companies and the lumbering firm jointly owned a large tract of land in and around Rhinelander. The New North explained "there has never been known an instance before where a railroad company offered a bonus to a competing line to enter its own territory. But the Lake Shore Company saw the feasibility of this step, knowing it would increase the value of their lands as well as the business of the town (New North, December 8, 1892, p.1)."

[25] New North, September 1, 1887, p.1, November 24, 1887, p.1, and December 1, 1887, p.1.

By the early 1890s the activities of the city's Business Men's Association stagnated and a new organization, The Rhinelander Advancement Association, was established. Although Eugene Shepard was not among the officers of this new association, he was a very active participant. Organized on May 1, 1891, the association endeavored to:

> promote the welfare and advancement of this city and county, by encouraging and securing manufacturing industries to locate here, furnishing sites for the same, and judiciously advertising the city, and in instances where circumstances will warrant granting bonuses.

The goals of the new association were similar to those of the B.M.A; however, the new organization used much more elaborate resources and techniques. While the B.M.A. was an informal organization that acted as a liaison between the city and would-be industrialists, the Rhinelander Advancement Association was organized as a corporation, selling fifty shares at $150 each in the spring of 1891. The R.A.A. invested part of its $7,500 bankroll in Rhinelander real estate, platting two manufacturing sites and approximately 120 residential lots. By December of the following year, the association had sold 75 residential lots and found itself in a position to offer dividends to its investors. Instead of paying dividends, however, the association chose to reinvest its capital in Rhinelander. Working with a bankroll and autonomy the B.M.A. never possessed, the R.A.A. achieved impressive results almost immediately.[26]

In 1891, J.A. Bruner and Edward A. Kemp decided after "great promotion by the Rhinelander Advancement Association" to relocate the Wabash Screen Door Company. The door company originated in Wabash, Indiana in 1885, but it quickly outgrew its location.

---

[26] "Rhinelander, part 3," <u>New North</u>, December 15, 1892, p.4.

Searching for a new location near pine and hardwood resources and adequately connected to rail transportation, Rhinelander impressed Bruner and Kemp. The R.A.A. donated ten acres of land on which the company constructed a three-story factory. With a capital stock of $30,000, the new factory began operations in October of 1891. By the following year, the company had grown to employ over 100 hands, and it produced 1,500 screen doors of nearly twenty different designs and material in a single day. By year's end, the company had produced over 224,000 doors, and it expected production to increase in 1893. According to the *New North*, it was the largest screen door factory in the world. More importantly for Rhinelander, the company paid a monthly payroll of nearly $6,000.[27]

The following year the Rhinelander Brewing Company and the Rhinelander Manufacturing Company (The Kirk Soap Company's box factory) both located in the city. Not all companies were offered the type of inducements the Wabash Screen Door Company received, however. The Rhinelander Brewing Company, for example, actually purchased the land on which it constructed its factory from the R.A.A. The association explained:

> because of the natural advantages of the area...[it didn't] deem it necessary to subsidize industries to any great extent, however, at the same time it will always lend aid and encouragement and in some instances where the circumstances warrant, will give sites and bonuses for the location of a factory.

The R.A.A. also endeavored to improve Rhinelander in other ways. It established an annual Oneida County Potato Show to help promote farming. It also established,

---

[27] Ibid., December 22, 1892, p.4; Lord, Industrial Review, 1898, 23; Vindicator, March 18, 1891, p.9, and April 22, 1891.

improved and maintained roads in and around Rhinelander - two of which were eventually designated state trunk highways. The association later became the city's chamber of commerce.[28]

By 1892 Rhinelander had begun to boost itself as "the banner city of Northern Wisconsin." Six years later, in the beginning of 1898, the city housed twelve manufacturing industries which employed 900 people (most related to the processing of pine lumber). With a population of 5,500 inhabitants, the city bragged of electric lights, a sewer system, water works, a police force, a paid three-company fire department, three weekly newspapers, nine churches, a twelve-grade public education system, railroad links in every direction with two major roads, and an advancement association to promote further growth. In addition, natural advantages blessed the city, not the least of which was the untapped water power of Pelican and Hat Rapids.[29]

Rhinelander's economy continued to be based primarily on lumber-related industry through the turn of the century. As businessmen thought of the future, they looked with anxiety to Rhinelander's post-lumbering days. Before 1900, however, any attempt to procure non-lumber related industry took a second seat to the more easily induced lumber industry. In the fall of 1896, Eugene Shepard became involved in a scheme that would possibly bridge the gap between the two. During the late 1890s, the Saint Paul Railway pushed north towards Rhinelander. Oneida County considered extending $20,000 worth of secured county bonds to the company to run the extension

[28] "Rhinelander, part 4," New North, December 22, 1893, p.1; "Rhinelander Brewing Company," New North, September 10, 1891, p.1; New North, April 14, 1892, p.1; Olsen, Our First Hundred Years, 70.

[29] "Rhinelander, part 1," New North, December 1, 1892, p.1; Lord, Industrial Review, 1898, 4-8.

through its county seat. Rhinelander, already serviced by the Chicago Northwestern and the Soo lines, was unsure if the benefits of a new rail connection warranted the tax increase the inducement required. The *New North* published two editorials on the subject. One, written by Eugene Shepard, urged the inducement be provided; the other, written by C.C. Yawkey, urged the inducement be rejected.[30]

Shepard based his argument on four premises, all directly related to lumbering, and one indirectly related to Rhinelander's upcoming post-lumber-boom days. First, the pine tracts opened by the railroad above Rhinelander would produce milling work for the city. Although most of the lands were owned by lumber barons outside of Rhinelander, Shepard pointed out that a good share of the land could easily be purchased by the city's lumber interests. Second, the building and traffic the railroad would bring would spur all sectors of local business. Third, the competition the new line would bring would pull down freight and passenger rates. Fourth, and most important to Rhinelander's future, the third railroad would give the city the best railroad connections throughout the whole northern region of the state. This would definitely play a role in inducing industrialists to move to the new city. In particular, it would make the water power available at Pelican Rapids more desirable for a paper milling firm.[31]

---

[30] New North, September 10, 1896, p.1. Although not nearly as extensive as the New North, the other city papers also printed several article in regard to the coming of the new railroad. See: Vindicator, July 18, 1896, p.4, and July 25, 1896, p.4; Rhinelander Herald, September 19, 1896, p.4. For a general discussion of railroad inducements in county development and the conflicts it involved regarding absentee tax payer's protests, see: Gates, The Wisconsin Pine Lands of Cornell University, 157, 177-207.

[31] New North, September 10, 1896, p.1.

Yawkey's rebuttal was equally convincing. He pointed out that the Saint Paul Railway might connect Rhinelander without receiving any inducements. In any event, Yawkey suggested that the railroad would not produce economic advantages for the city. It would be built with funds and supplies procured outside of the area, adding no significant advancement to the local economy. Furthermore, the other two railroads offered more direct routes to other economic sectors of the region; the new railroad would not drive down rates, or even be widely used by the local community. Yawkey also pointed out that most of the timber open by the Saint Paul Railway would be processed in other cities as it was owned by men with established milling sites elsewhere. The protest concluded that it wasn't worth the increased tax burden on the already over-taxed inhabitants of the county.[32]

Both Shepard and Yawkey inferred that the other had a vested interest in the outcome. Yawkey suggested that the Goodyear company, a company that owned much of the timber to be opened by the railroad and one that Shepard was still closely associated with, would be the only true beneficiary. Shepard likewise suggested Yawkey was an agent of the Soo Line, a company that "discriminated against us in their local passenger rates." It seems both of these attacks were unwarranted, and both men acted on a belief that their position was the best for Rhinelander, regardless of who else might benefit. Oneida County never offered the bonds, and Rhinelander never received the third connection. The city remained, however, as Yawkey pointed out, with "two roads...and...better fixed than most cities in this respect."[33]

As the turn of the century neared, Rhinelander

---

[32] Ibid., September 10, 1896, p.1.

[33] Ibid., September 10, 1896, p.1, and September 17, 1896, p.1; Jones, History of Lincoln, Oneida, and Vilas Counties, 113.

continued its attempt to diversify.   The most obvious strategy involved harvesting and processing the previously neglected hardwoods of the area.   In an 1898 industrial review of the city, Alman Lord insisted that the turn of the century would bring a "metamorphosis of the city.   She will gradually change from pine lumber producer to a manufacturer of other lines such as furnishings, wagon materials, etc., drawing on the almost inexhaustible supply of hardwood tributary."   By the turn of the century, the lumbering heyday was quickly passing.   The year 1899 witnessed the closing of four of Rhinelander's eight sawmills.   What began as a source of anxiety in 1887 became a source of panic in 1900.[34]

In the summer of 1902, Shepard, working within the advancement association, continued actively soliciting manufacturing for Rhinelander.   In June of that year, Shepard and two others met with a New York industrialist who considered relocating his pail manufacturing plant. Although in August the venture seemed like it would materialize, the industrialist never established his plant in Rhinelander.   At the same time Shepard himself decided to try his hand at manufacturing.   Through his connections to Chicago's Union League Club, Shepard entered into a joint venture with Chicago investors.   The partnership, utilizing Shepard's building on Davenport Street, shipped in machinery from Chicago to produce "builder's hardware, such as locks, trimmings, [and] window fastenings."   The *New North* expressed appreciation that men like Shepard chose "to remain and invest their money where they made it," instead of following the lumbering trade west.[35]

The work at Shepard's factory commenced nicely

---

[34]   Olsen, Our First hundred Years, 52, 70; Lord, Industrial Review, 4-8; Kortenhof, Sugar Camp, 17.

[35]   New North, June 19, 1902, p.1, and June 19, 1902, p.1; "A New Industry," Rhinelander Herald, June 21, 1902, p.4.

through July, and in early August the venture expected to begin turning out locks within the month. Unfortunately, the factory struggled. By March of 1904, Shepard cleared out the manufacturing equipment and remodeling the' location for retail. That autumn, Shepard opened the New Fair Store, employing ten people in a store which appeared to be "the neatest in the city being decorated in a manner most elaborate and artistic." Despite its original promise, the Fair Store, like the factory that preceded it, did not endure.[36]

A different vision of Shepard's did eventually materialize and endure. Since early 1902, Shepard had been publicly stressing the need to develop the untapped water power at Hat Rapids (about six miles south of Rhinelander on the Wisconsin River). By December of 1903, Shepard and A.W. Shelton "were granted a charter for...the organization of a stock company to carry out the plan..." In February of 1904 the Rhinelander Power Company incorporated for that purpose. Although the company elected A.W. Shelton president, it did not list Shepard among the incorporators. The company completed a 140-foot hydroelectric dam across the Wisconsin River at Hat Rapids in 1905. Three 11,000-volt Bullock generators provided power at the facility, and an alternating electrical current, produced by the rapids' water power, supplied the city of Rhinelander. This facility was the first of its kind built in the nation. Although Shepard was not among the company's incorporators he was the catalyst that made the dam a possibility. In December of 1903, before the Rhinelander Power Company was even established, the *New North* proclaimed: "For a number of years has the improvement of the water power at Hat Rapids been the dominant thought in the resourceful mind of E.S. Shepard." The power plant eventually served the surrounding cities in

---

[36] New North, July 10, 1902, p.1, August 7, 1902, p.5, March 24, 1904, p.5, and September 22, 1904, p.1.

addition to Rhinelander.[37]

While Shepard involved himself in these projects, the city of Rhinelander crossed the bridge from lumbering boomtown to industrial city. Early in 1902, the Wabash Screen Door factory burned to the ground and its proprietor, E.A. Kemp, decided not to rebuild. His decision devastated the city. The local papers repeatedly called it a most crucial time in Rhinelander's short history, and they pleaded for the city's business community to act in unison to procure outside investment. The following excerpts from the August 28th, 1902 issue of the *New North* illustrate the crisis the city perceived:

> Until Rhinelander is back to where it was when the screen door factory burned it can afford to give one hundred dollars for every permanently employed for ten years. We must have something to take the institutions place.

> Rhinelander is sick. Its vitality is low. It will grow healthy again if there is injected into it a solution of progress and enterprise. A couple of new factories will revive the patient.

> A factory giving steady employment to 50 men is worth more to Rhinelander today than one employing twice that number will be a few years from now.

The despair of Autumn 1902 was replaced with unbounded enthusiasm in February of 1903. The untapped water power of Pelican Rapids and the superior shipping connections of Rhinelander's two railroads paved the way for the establishment of a paper mill. The Chicago and Northwestern Railroad agreed to donate their interest in the rapids and the Brown family joyfully donated their half. The city contracted an Oshkosh firm to construct the mill and Rhinelander investors amassed $100,000 for the project. The mill, which even today remains the city's

---

[37] Ibid., December 24, 1903, p.1, and February 25, 1904, p.5, Olsen, Our First Hundred Years, 81.

largest employer, couldn't have been established at a better time. The *Vindicator* exclaimed in boldface: "Build Paper Mill: Two hundred hands will be given employment - A great thing for the city - Water power will be developed and other industries will follow." The *New North* was equally enthusiastic and printed the headline: "The Star of Rhinelander is Rising: Never before was there such a splendid outlook for the future of a city as now faces our Rhinelander." What Shepard had worked for ten years earlier had finally been established, and it, like the lumber mills before it, served as a economic base for the city.[38]

Shepard continued to plan his personal investment in Rhinelander throughout the first decade of the twentieth century. Early in 1906, he purchased two lots fronting Davenport Street and announced plans to erect an extravagant 40'x80' two-story office building. Each of the five office suites would house a storage closet and a fire proof vault. The basement was to become an athletic club complete with a heated pool. At the same time Shepard purchased a lot on Stevens Street on which he intended to erect a hotel. 1906 would prove to be a very busy year for Shepard, as he spent three months vacationing on the West Coast, purchased a new home, and ran for two political offices. The year never saw the construction of the office building or the hotel, however, and Shepard discarded his plans.[39]

Later in 1906 Shepard attempted to re-enter the political arena with bids for the positions of city mayor and state assemblyman. Toward the end of January, 1906, Rhinelander Mayor Matt Stapleton announced that he would not run for reelection, stating that "some other good

---

[38] New North, February 5, 1903, p.1; "Build Paper Mill," Vindicator, January 31, 1903, p.1; Olsen, Our First Hundred Years, 63.

[39] Vindicator, January 10, 1906, p.5.

citizen should take upon himself and his family the abuse that my family and I have taken in the last two years." Ignoring Stapleton's sarcastic warning, Shepard announced his candidacy on the first of February and was soon challenged by former Mayor Fred Anderle and prominent businessman Alex McRae.   The *New North*, which normally showed Shepard in a favorable light, offered at best a lukewarm endorsement.   After hinting that his announcement might be "another josh," the paper found it difficult to speak highly of Shepard, printing: "We might tell of Mr. Shepard's many virtues etc., but we don't know of any, and he probably hasn't any, unless confidence in Rhinelander could be called a virtue, and he has that and always has had it." The article recounted Shepard's efforts to secure a right-of-way for the Chicago Minneapolis & St. Paul and added that it was "no fault of his" that the railroad did not run through Rhinelander. The paper half-heartedly concluded: "...should the people desire him for mayor this Spring the duties of the office would be discharged conscientiously."[40]

The following month it became clear that the *New North* preferred Anderle; the paper published a favorable account of him as it announced his filing of nomination papers.   Shortly   thereafter   the   city's   Scandinavian Republican Club endorsed Anderle. It seems that none of the three candidates campaigned very diligently, as McRae's name was not even mentioned in the *New North* until it reported the election results (the *Vindicator* announced   McRae's   candidacy   on   March   21). Furthermore, Shepard left for Chicago and shortly thereafter embarked on a three-month pleasure trip to the West Coast.   The election results clearly reflected Shepard's failure to receive an endorsement, his lack of campaigning, and his absence from town throughout the

---

[40]   Ibid., January 31, 1906, p.5; New North, February 1, 1906, p.1, and April 3, 1906, p.1.

entire process.   Anderle secured a landslide victory,
capturing 784 votes.   He out-polled his competitors by
nearly a three-to-one margin.   McRae followed Anderle
with 204 votes. Shepard returned to Rhinelander a month
after the election to find he had received only 30 votes and
finished a distant last.[41]

Just over a month after Shepard's crushing defeat in
the mayoral race, the *New North* published a front page
article encouraging him to run for assemblyman of the 53rd
district representing Oneida, Vilas and Iron counties.
Shepard's   popularity   and   political   and   economic
connections throughout the state prompted the paper to "go
on record as making the statement that [if Shepard entered
the assembly race] he will be elected."   The paper
contended that "no man is better known in Vilas, Oneida
and Iron counties than Gene Shepard," who is known to
"every man women and child in this district."[42]   The
following week Shepard officially announced his candidacy.
In an advertisement that ran the duration of the campaign
Shepard stated:

> I hereby announce myself a candidate for the nomination to
> the office of assemblyman in the 53rd district consisting of the
> territories of Oneida, Iron and Vilas counties. I have lived in
> the territory twenty-four years and have been a land cruiser
> thirty-six years. I would very respectfully ask my friends to
> support me which would be very much appreciated.[43]

Two weeks later A.M. Riley announced he intended to
challenge Shepard in the Republican primary.   Although

---

[41]   Ibid., February 8, 1906, p.5, March 8, 1906, p.1, March
22, 1906, p.1, and April 3, 1906, p.1; Vindicator, January 31,
1906, p.5, March 21, 1906, p.1, and April 4, 1906, p.1.

[42]   New North, May 31, 1906, p.1.

[43]   Ibid., June 7, 1906, p.1.

Riley eventually dropped out of the race, the Eagle River incumbent Edward A. Everett replaced his challenge. In addition, Rhinelander's Herman Zander ran on the Social Democrat ticket. With Zander failing to offer a serious threat to the Republican ticket and the Democrats not forwarding a candidate, the September 4th primary became the *de facto* election. Shepard carried Rhinelander by capturing a 250 vote majority, but Everett made up ground in Eagle River and the rest of the district. The election was so tight that it took over three weeks to calculate the results. In the confusion immediately following the vote, the *Vindicator* actually announced Shepard's victory by "a small majority." In the end, however, the *Vindicator*'s announcement and the *New North*'s prediction proved incorrect and Shepard lost to his Eagle River opponent by a slight margin.[44]

Despite Shepard's failed political endeavors, he continued to represent Oneida County in several voluntary booster organizations, including the Northern Wisconsin Farmer's Association. This association, organized by the counties to the north of Oneida, promoted the transition of cut-over lands to agricultural areas. In May of 1906, an elaborate train car pulled into Rhinelander for a two-hour layover. The car, dubbed the "Grassland," was the advertising vehicle of the N.W.F.A. The outside of the car was equipped with glass-plated show cases below and between the windows; these cases displayed "wheat, oats, barley, flax[,] buckwheat and rye, timothy, alfalfa, clover and bluegrass all of which came from Northern Wisconsin soil." The inside of the car was decorated with photographs of farms, buildings, schools, fair exhibits, churches, and businesses from the northern districts of

---

[44] Ibid., June 21, 1906, p.1, August 16, 1906, p.8, September 6, 1906, p.4, September 13, 1906, p.4, and September 27, 1906, p.8; Vindicator, July 25, 1906, p.8. For false announcement see: Vindicator, September 5, 1906, p.4.

Wisconsin.   The traveling exhibit made an instant
impression on the people of Rhinelander, and they quickly
raised the $500.00 membership fee and joined the
association.   In August of 1906,   Shepard, along with
Charles Chafee, received an appointment to Oneida
County's Executive Committee of the Northern Wisconsin
Farmer's Association.   When the "Grassland" returned to
Rhinelander the following October, it proudly displayed
Oneida County's exhibit in the center of the car.   The car
then embarked on an advertising trip to the central states of
Illinois, Iowa, Indiana and Ohio.[45]

In November of the following year, Shepard was
elected vice president of the Northern Wisconsin
Development Association.   This organization worked
closely with the newly created State Board of Immigration
to promote immigration to the northern counties of
Wisconsin.   The organization immediately "sent out a
lecturer equipped with a stereopticon and views illustrating
the agricultural and industrial resources of the counties
represented in the Association."   The organization routinely
exhibited agricultural produce and "liberally dished out"
literature describing the counties.   The day before Shepard
was elected vice president he penned a lengthy article in
the *New North* explaining the need to "boost northern
Wisconsin" and the specific role the N.W.D.A. intended to
play.   Shepard explained:

> The movement to organize the Northern Wisconsin counties
> for the purpose of cooperating with the state board of
> immigration has met with hearty enthusiasm and County
> development associations in nearly all northern counties have
> been organized with the view of securing appropriations from
> their respective Counties and assisting in the work of
> promoting immigration...a federation known as The North
> Wisconsin Development Association was organized.   This

---

[45]   New North, August 2, 1906, p.1; Vindicator, May 23,
1906, p.1, and October 17, 1906, p.1.

organization provides a means of organized and systematic work.[46]

In addition to these county-based associations, Shepard also involved himself with the re-emergence of the Rhinelander Business Men's Association. Early in 1909, the association was re-founded and held its "first annual meeting." In mid-June of that same year, Shepard, along with C.A. Wixson, addressed the members of the association in a lecture focusing on the importance of soliciting new settlers for Rhinelander. Early the following year, Shepard served as part of a B.M.A. delegation formed to travel to Chicago and meet with the owners of a large office furniture manufacture who had expressed interest in relocating to Rhinelander.[47]

Even while Shepard vigorously promoted Rhinelander, he dabbled with the idea of leaving the city for the opportunities he saw further north. His first venture was the failed speculation effort at Hannaford, Minnesota, discussed previously. Shepard's other venture from Rhinelander met a similar fate. Around the turn of the century, apparently discouraged by the waning lumber industry and the increasing distance he was forced to travel

---

[46] New North, December 19, 1907, p.1; Eugene Shepard, "Boost Northern Wisconsin," New North, November 28, 1907, p.1,8. Previously Shepard was active in the Oneida County Immigration Society, of which he remained active through the final years of his life (E.S. Shepard to W.E. Nuzum, December 20, 1922; the return address on the envelope read: Oneida County Immigration Society, E.S. Shepard Sec'y). These county organizations, and the N.W.D.A. were supported by appropriations of county boards of up to $1,000 per year, under Chapter 458 Laws of 1905. For example, Forest and Oneida Counties each allocated $500 for the support of the N.W.D.A. in 1907 (New North, December 19, 1907, p.1).

[47] New North, February 24, 1910, p.1, June 17, 1909, p.1, and February 3, 1910, p.1.

to practice his trade, Shepard attempted to exploit another aspect of the northwoods. During the Spring of 1900, he converted a summer cabin at Star Lake, Wisconsin into an elaborate summer resort. The resort, named "The House of the Good Shepard," opened for business on June 10, 1900.[48]

Star Lake, located 17 miles northwest of Eagle River, Wisconsin, was a lumbering boomtown surrounded by Ballard, Irving, Laura, Rice, Razorback, and Plum Lakes. Established by the Williams and Salisch Lumber Company, Star Lake evolved from virgin forest to a boomtown over night. The tiny hamlet housed 600 inhabitants, hotels, churches, a school, and a post office. The town became the Chicago, Milwaukee & St. Paul Railway's northernmost terminus after the lumber company struck a deal with the railroad to extend to the location. Beginning in 1895, peaking in 1901 and 1902, and rapidly declining after the company pulled out in 1906, Star Lake serves as a classic example of a bustling lumber boomtown turned ghost town.[49]

Shepard attempted to exploit the natural beauty and advantages of the region (and that it was directly linked via rail to Chicago and Milwaukee) by erecting a pleasure resort on Ballard Lake. He was not the first to attempt this, in fact the Williams and Salisch Lumber Company

---

[48] "The Greatest Muskellunge Fishing in the World; Address: E.S. Shepard, Star Lake, Vilas County, Wisconsin," Promotional handbill published by Shepard, 1900.

[49] Jones, History of Lincoln, Oneida, and Vilas Counties, 203-4; Randall Rohe, "Star Lake: From Boom Town to Ghost Town," in Proceedings of Seventeenth Annual Meeting of Forest History Association of Wisconsin (Eagle River, Wisconsin, 1992), 37-45. For a general history of Star Lake see also: Cecelia Ellerman, This Land The Way It Was (Sayner - Star Lake) (Star Lake, 1983); and for a mix of history and fiction, Ellerman, The Resort People (Star Lake, 1989).

operated an elaborate resort and hotel during its stay in the region. Shepard's promotional material read:

> **House of the Good Shepard on Ballard Lake Vilas Co**
> This new summer home will be open to the public June 10th 1900.   It is situated on Ballard Lake which is the best muskellunge lake in the state. The Bass, Pike and all kinds of fishing is so good here as the most enthusiastic could desire. The resort is surrounded by upwards of 20 fine lakes teaming with all kinds of fish, and are reached by boat through channels connecting them and Indian trails crossing from one lake to the other...My boats are new clean and roomy... My guides are all well posted on the fishing grounds and are sober and thoroughly reliable. There will be a toboggan slide in operation on the premises upon which to slide down about 200 ft into the lake in shallow water which is a very excitable pass time... Fine cottages on the premises for families. Notify me at Star Lake Vilas Co Wis when you will arrive and transportation will await you to bring you to the resort 2 1/2 miles from the Depot. Hoping to meet you here during the season, I am Yours Truly,
> E.S. Shepard[50]

This promotion appeared on a handbill, distributed in Chicago and Milwaukee. A map of the region and drawing of the resort accompanied the handbill (see figure 3.1).

In addition to this handbill, Shepard received some publicity from an expanded article appearing in the August 18, 1900 edition of the *Chicago Evening Post.* An article entitled "Mid Virgin Forests" claimed that the natural beauty of Star Lake brought "out one's better side and make[s] him think that, after all, the world is not all bad." The article also spoke of the abundance of fish and game. Although signed "the Student," it seems logical that Shepard wrote the piece or at least played an active role in

---

[50] Shepard, "The Greatest Muskellunge Fishing in the World."

its conception.[51]

Shepard's initial season as a resort operator proved to be his last; he sold his resort, which was then renamed Fencroft, in the same year it was opened. Shepard's ventures in Hannaford and Star Lake thus proved failures, and he remained in Rhinelander for the rest of his life. Shepard's experiences in these areas represent an interesting contradiction. While actively boosting Rhinelander, Shepard also seriously contemplated leaving the city for new opportunities. In the case of the Star Lake resort this contradiction is not as strong because it appears that the resort was strictly a summer operation and Shepard probably planned to reside in Rhinelander during the off-season. In the case of Hannaford, however, things are not as easy to explain; Shepard's endeavors in Northern Minnesota occurred at the same time he energetically boosted Rhinelander.

By 1909, Shepard began to fade from public view, and by 1911 he played a very quiet role in city social life and politics (possibly because he was confronted with illness and personal difficulties that led to divorce and remarriage in the oncoming years). For whatever reason, Shepard's voice, with few exceptions, was noticeably absent from local affairs after 1911. In fact, upon selling his house on Pelham Street in January of that year, the *New North* incorrectly suggested that Shepard had intended to leave Wisconsin and follow the lumber industry west.[52]

Shepard's activity in and on behalf of Rhinelander from 1882 through the first decade of the twentieth century offers insight into turn-of-the-century localized public

---

[51] "Mid Virgin Forest; Beauties and Attractions Found in Northern Wisconsin; Lumber Jack Superstitions; Shepard and His Wonderful Hodag Which Hoodwinked the Natives and Others for Years," Chicago Evening Post, August 18, 1900, p.4.

[52] "Excellent Property Sells," New North, January 12, 1911, p.1.

policy. The events and policies pursued in Rhinelander were not unique or extraordinary; rather they mirrored what was going on throughout the state, region, and country. In this sense Rhinelander offers a solid example of turn-of-the-century boosterism. Shepard's lack of success in certain endeavors should not distract from his contribution to Rhinelander and its development. His involvement in the various boosting organization certainly contributed to Rhinelander's advance. Furthermore, many of the ideas which he failed to realize were eventually achieved by others that followed his lead. The development of waterpower at Hat Rapids and the securing of the paper mill are the two best examples.

Judged by their own standards, the boosters of Rhinelander were successful; the city overcame the closing of the lumbering era. The population of Rhinelander continued to grow steadily, reaching its apex of 8,790 in 1960 before falling off slightly the following decades. More importantly, around the turn of the century Rhinelander successfully diversified its industrial complex. In writings towards the end of his life, Shepard explained the progress he witnessed and the role early settlers played in the realization of that progress:

> comfortable homes on large, stumpless farms have taken the place of virgin pine; automobiles travel on good road where, a few years ago I travelled with my pack-sack on a not-too-well travelled trail or no trail at all...[53] Rhinelander prospered and we thank those early settlers one and all for their backing and good will in making a city of Rhinelander. Truly men make towns and ever will so long as they can agree among themselves as we all did.[54]

Today, surrounded by communities solely dependant on

---

[53] Shepard and Shepard, Paul Bunyan, 11-12.

[54] Shepard, "Reminiscences," New North, December 12, 1912.

tourism, Rhinelander continues to act as the regional industrial center of north-central Wisconsin. How much of this success was due to the efforts of Eugene S. Shepard is difficult to determine, but that he was a influential part of the processes is certain.

Figure 2.1: Shepard's illustration of his Star Lake, Wisconsin resort "House of the Good Shepard." Promotional handbill, 1900.

CHAPTER III

LOCAL COLOR: PRANKS AND PERSONALITY

Although Shepard's posts in local government and activity in various booster organizations probably had the greatest influence on the development of Rhinelander, it is his personality and humor for which he is remembered. Shepard had an extraordinary imagination and a phenomenal ability to communicate his ideas to others; he spoke, wrote and drew with great skill. His imagination, when coupled with impressive communication skills, was employed with great success in his work in the land trade and in his endeavors to promote Rhinelander. Unfortunately, often his humor was misguided or overdone, and despite a love of people, he found himself at times alienated from a local population that tired of his antics. Furthermore, Shepard's relationship with his family was always strained and at times extremely difficult.

Well before Rhinelander's founding, Shepard discovered an outlet for his unusual talents within the lumber industry. When evaluating timber tracts near operating lumber camps, cruising crews often paid a small room-and-board fee and stayed in company bunkhouses. Shepard took advantage of this hospitality and often frequented lumber camps throughout northern Minnesota, Wisconsin and Michigan. In these bunkhouses Shepard perfected the art of storytelling and gained a reputation that made him arguably the best-known cruiser in the region.

The lumber camps throughout the Midwest were seldom filled with the stereotypical collections of rosy-faced lumberjacks telling stories around a comforting woodstove. "The romance of the logging camps," as Robert Nesbit points out, "makes light of vermin-infested clothes, unwashed bodies, animal and human waste as part of the immediate landscape, and crowded living with nowhere to go." The turn-of-the-century lumber industry was one of the poorest paying, ranking 24th of the 25 major industries in Wisconsin in 1887-1888, and most hazardous of all American industries. However, isolated in the dead of winter, confined to tight quarters and having nothing to do after finishing the evening meal, the lumberjacks did indeed tell stories to pass the time. Luke Kearney probably did not exaggerate when he stated: "it was in the bunkhouses of the American lumber camps that the art of storytelling reached its peak." These lumberjack stories, never told the same twice, almost always focused on the feats of mythical creatures and industry heros. That a true North American folklore was born and perpetuated in the lumber camps of the continent cannot be denied, and that the supreme mythical character was Paul Bunyan is equally apparent. Eugene Shepard flourished in this environment, and his popularity as a storyteller certainly was the basis for his reputation as one of the best-known timber cruisers in the Midwest.[1]

Paul Bunyan may have been the name of an industrious New England lumberjack, but it is just as possible that the man never existed. The importance of Bunyan is not whether his origin is based on an authentic lumberjack or just a figment of the imagination, but rather what he became - the premier character in North American

---

[1] Nesbit, Urbanization and Industrialization, 1873-1893 vol 3, History of Wisconsin, 62-63, 72; Luke Sylvester Kearney, The Hodag: And Other Tales of the Logging Camps (Wausau, Wisconsin, 1928), 4.

folklore. Bunyan stories probably first appeared during the middle of the nineteenth century and by 1895 the lumber camps of western Pennsylvania and New York knew Bunyan well. Bunyan stories quickly flourished and followed the lumber industry west across the United States and Canada. Originally Bunyan was nothing more than an "occupational hero," confined to the bunkhouses of the lumber camps. Unlike his counterparts (Pecos Bill, John Henry, etc...), Bunyan began to appear in the pages of newspapers and trade magazines by the first decade of the twentieth century. During the 1920s, Bunyan stories became popular topics in national newspapers and magazines, soon thereafter full-length books recounting the exploits of the mythical lumberjack emerged. Bunyan, possibly because the lumber industry was not confined to any one region of North America, transcended his occupational origins and became a folk hero of a continent.[2]

The Bunyan that Shepard and his counterparts spoke of around the woodstoves was different than the hero that eventually emerged in the literature of popular culture. The original oral stories were less refined or suitable for mass consumption and filled with extensive references to industry-specific language - references the layman would not understand. Both Bunyans, however, possessed what

---

[2] Daniel Hoffman, Paul Bunyan: Last of the Frontier Demigods (Philadelphia, 1952), 1, 165, 2; K. Bernice Stewart and Homer A. Watt, "Legends of Paul Bunyan, Lumberjack," Transactions of the Wisconsin Academy of Sciences, Arts and Letters 18, part 2, (1916): 641-42. The subject of Paul Bunyan has been extensively covered by vast amounts of secondary literature, an adequate survey of which is far beyond the scope of this study. For a solid analytical account of Bunyan's role in American folklore form his occupational origins to his emergence in popular culture and a well-developed bibliography of his treatment in secondary literature see: Hoffman, Paul Bunyan: Last of the Frontier Demigods (Philadelphia, 1952).

the lumberjacks believed to be qualities of a hero. For their hero the woodsman choose one of their own, made him large, humorous, clever and equipped him with an equally impressive blue ox, Babe. Bunyan could think and work his way out of any bind a lumber crew might find itself in. The lumberjacks found something comforting in the custom of believing (or pretending to believe) in the mythical hero. Bunyan transcended mere humor and came to embody the ideals of those who cherished him. Although superhuman, Bunyan was "created in the image of human aspirations;" he embodied the personal conduct, ethical code, and goals of the lumbermen who spoke of him.[3]

Shepard told and retold of the exploits of Paul Bunyan as he witnessed them while a member of Bunyan's crew.[4] Employed as a timber cruiser for the Brown Brothers Lumber Company, Martin Fitzgerald witnessed Shepard's storytelling first hand:

> As the lumberjacks sat around the bunkhouse evenings, listening to stories, 'Gene' Shepard was their conception of Paul Bunyan. I knew Shepard well, I can see him now sitting in the chair, with one leg crossed over the other, with the upright foot tossing back and forth as he talked.
>
> 'Gene' was a heavy man with a happy, round face which reflected his thoughts as he related his yarns. I have heard him repeat stories, but they were never the same as the original telling. Always he added new particulars and amplified with greater details of astonishment the story at each unfolding. I think more fascinating episodes in Bunyan tales originated with 'Gene' Shepard than in any other mind.... Shepard may have obtained the original idea from some other lumberjack, but the listener would never recognize the creation

---

[3] Hoffman, Paul Bunyan, viii.

[4] It was customary for all Bunyan storytellers to claim they had worked on Bunyan's crew and that they witnessed Bunyan's exploits first-hand.

after Shepard's second telling, so marvelous were the circumstances supplied.[5]

In 1929 Shepard's second wife, Karretta Gunderson Shepard, posthumously published a short volume of Shepard's stories. *Paul Bunyan: His Camp and Wife*, is "a sketch of Paul Bunyan's life, from the beginning of his logging days to the time of his retirement to his country seat, and other woods stories told by Eugene S. Shepard, put into verse by Karretta Gunderson Shepard." The volume of poetry, which also includes "some favorite songs of the old-time lumberjacks," offers an understanding of the type of stories Shepard spread through the pineries. It does not, however, capture the presentation style that Fitzgerald contends made Shepard popular in the bunkhouses.[6]

Inevitable drawbacks notwithstanding, *Paul Bunyan: His Camp and Wife* does offer insight into various aspects of Shepard's character. Shepard's sense of humor is clearly present, as the poems often center on the practical pranks Shepard played on unsuspecting "greenhorns" (a common practice of the seasoned woodsmen). In addition, the publication is extensively illustrated with Shepard's pen-and-ink drawings. The drawings not only illustrate

---

[5] Martin Fitzgerald as quoted in Fred Holmes, <u>Badger Saints and Sinners</u> (Milwaukee, 1938), 472-73. Holmes annotated this quotation with the following note: "This view of the authorship of Bunyan stories was confirmed by many personal acquaintances of Shepard who enjoyed his companionship in logging operations in Northern Wisconsin."

[6] Eugene S. Shepard and Karretta Gunderson Shepard, <u>Paul Bunyan: His Camp and Wife</u> (Tomahawk, Wisconsin, 1929). Published by a local press, this volume never became widely known; it is not mentioned in any of the studies of Paul Bunyan lore I have consulted. Today the book is extremely rare. The University of Wisconsin-Madison library and the Rhinelander Historical Society, however, each own a copy.

Shepard's competence as a amateur artist, but also his humor and his ability to use this skill to explain his stories, advertise his land agency and promote Rhinelander (see figures 3.1 through 3.3).

Interestingly, "The Round River Drive" is conspicuously absent from *Paul Bunyan: His Camp and Wife*. Shepard claimed authorship of this lengthy poem that recounted Paul Bunyan and his crew's efforts to drive logs down a round river. The poem also appeared in the April 25th, 1914 edition of the *American Lumberman* (a national trade journal) which credited its composition to Douglas Malloch. The two versions of the poem are virtually identical with only minor discrepancies dealing with location and the names of the lumberjacks who later revisited Bunyan's Round River camp. In Shepard's version, the Round River is located 50 miles west of Rhinelander; while in Malloch's, the ill-fated drive took place 50 miles west of Graylin, Michigan.[7]

It is not known whether the first prints of Shepard's poem, published by the C.C. Collins Lumber Company of Rhinelander, appeared before the 1914 printing of Malloch's version. There is, however, ample evidence that suggests Shepard plagiarized Malloch's creation and not vice versa. First, the fact that Shepard's widow failed to include the poem, which was perhaps more popular than

---

[7] Shepard's version of the poem was printed and distributed around Rhinelander by the C.C. Collins Lumber Company. The Rhinelander Logging Museum and the State Historical Society of Wisconsin both own original copies of the printing. In addition, Shepard's version is reprinted in full in Luke Kearney, The Hodag: And Other Tales of the Lumber Camps (Wausau, Wisconsin, 1928), 18-28; an abbreviated version may be found in Robert E. Gard and L.G. Sorden, Wisconsin Lore (Sauk City, Wisconsin, 1976), 77-80. Malloch's version first appeared in the American Lumberman (April 25, 1914) and has been reprinted in numerous Bunyan publications including Harold W. Felton, Legends of Paul Bunyan (New York, 1947), 341-50.

Shepard's hodag, in *Paul Bunyan: His Camp and Wife* suggests that she knew Shepard was not the authentic author. Second, only people living around Rhinelander or personally acquainted with Shepard have credited the poem to his hand. Third, Layton Shepard, Eugene's youngest son, admitted that "a Milwaukee man named Clark helped [his father] write the poem." Furthermore, in a 1922 letter Shepard himself insinuated that the poem was not a product of his own creation. Referring to the Round River Poem, Shepard wrote Judge A.H. Reid of Wausau, Wisconsin: "I am inclosing [*sic*] the story the American Lumberman poet helped me get into rhyme." That Shepard did not refer to Malloch by name suggests that the men were not personally acquainted. The evidence, although not conclusive, suggests that Shepard read Malloch's poem in the *American Lumberman*, made a few alterations, and passed it off locally as his own.[8]

Regardless of the implications of Shepard's use of Malloch's material, it is clear the latter brought the lumber camp traditions of storytelling and practical pranking with him when he moved to Rhinelander. From the city's conception Shepard became the community jester and most extravagant entertainer. The locals soon learned that a good story may be heard at Shepard's land office and a city paper reported his artistic ability writing: "E.S. Shepard, crayon artist, portrait work a specialty." Shepard's stories and pranks became legendary in and around Rhinelander; as he entertained the lumberjacks, he began to entertain the townspeople.[9]

Versions of Shepard's numerous tall tales are still

---

[8] Jack Cory, Jack Cory's Scrapbook (Lake Tomahawk, Wisconsin), 7; E.S. Shepard to Judge A.H. Reid, n.d., reprinted in "Mrs. Paul Bunyan Even More Resourceful Than Her Husband," New North, May 11, 1922, p.1.

[9] New North, March 4, 1886, p.1.

present in Rhinelander and account for an important element of the area's local color. Although Shepard always stretched the truth, some, if not most, of his stories were founded in an element of reality. For example, Shepard often told of his run-in with "a wild Kentuckian" in a tavern north of Crandon, Wisconsin. According to Shepard, the southerner was on a drunken tirade threatening the saloon patrons with his rifle as he bragged of the men he killed. Shepard and his companion, Matt Stapleton, concocted a scheme to rid the tavern of the madman and acquire his rifle and lantern. Stapleton feigned he was infected with rabies and bit the Kentuckian. The plan was successful and the man fled. The Kentuckian left behind his rifle and lantern which Shepard and Stapleton quickly commandeered. Granting some credence to the story, the September 17th, 1903 issue of the *New North* carried an article detailing an altercation in a saloon just north of Crandon, which ended with gunfire. Ezra Comb, the gunman from Kentucky escaped after wounding one man and killing another. It is possible that Shepard and Stapleton were in the saloon at the time of the altercation, or it is just as likely that Shepard read the story in the local paper and turned it into one of his fabricated exploits. In either case, Shepard's version of the account has survived the years, and has made its way into several publications.[10]

---

[10] "Kentuckian Uses Revolver," New North, September 17, 1903, p.1. For Shepard's version of the altercation see: Gard and Sorden, Wisconsin Lore, 249-50 and Dave Peterson, Hodag: A New Musical Based on the Exploits of Gene Shepard, Wisconsin's Greatest Trickster (Madison, 1964), 12-18. Many versions of Shepard's tales are recounted in local literature, see: Gard and Sorden, Wisconsin Lore; Peterson, Hodag: A New Musical; Shepard, Paul Bunyan; Holmes, Badger Saints and Sinners. Also contemporary accounts of Shepard Stories were often printed in local papers. For examples see: "Shep Tells This. The North Western Sportsman Hears From The Hodag Man," Vindicator, February 14,

In addition to storytelling, Shepard also brought the prankster mentality of the lumber camps to Rhinelander. Although his pranks were as numerous as his far-fetched stories, two examples of his most famous serve to explain' the character and purpose of these practical jokes. Upon returning from an extended cruising trip, Shepard announced he discovered a rare form of "scented moss." Devising a ploy that lasted two years, Shepard charged tourists $.25 to smell the exotic moss. There are even stories of Shepard, in cooperation with a Rhinelander women's organization, selling the moss (via mail-order) to customers down state and as far south as Chicago. The moss became a drawing card for Shepard's Star Lake resort, the House of the Good Shepard, during the summer of 1900. The ploy was later exposed as ordinary moss treated with a heavy dose of cheap perfume. Shepard also hood-winked the guests at his resort with an imitation muskellunge. At times the fishing on Ballard Lake was not "The Greatest Muskellunge Fishing in the World" as Shepard's promotional material promised. To remedy the situation, Shepard, through a system of wires, caused his imitation fish to repeatedly jump from the water. This ploy often impressed the guests enough to renew their reservations for an extended stay.[11]

The scented moss and the imitation muskellunge, along with countless other pranks, gave Shepard a

---

1906, p.5; "E.S. Shepard Had Quite A Fishing Experience," Vindicator, August 28, 1890, p.4.

[11] "Hoax Alive and Well: Hodag Fooled Some People for a Time," Wisconsin Then and Now 22, no. 1, (August, 1975): 6; "Fate of Terrible Hodag Cleared Up At Last," Sentinel Sunday Magazine, May 27, 1923, p.5; Gard and Sorden, Wisconsin Lore, 252-53; Shepard, Paul Bunyan, 53-54; Holmes, Badger Saints and Sinners, 468-69; "Greatest Muskellunge Fishing in the World," Shepard promotional handbill, 1900. For other pranks refer to literature mentioned in preceding footnote.

reputation as the P.T. Barnum of Northern Wisconsin. Often, as was the case with the moss and the muskellunge, Shepard's pranks were intended to produce financial gain, or business promotion in addition to provoking a good laugh. In semi-retirement after 1906, Shepard filled his den, a brick structure constructed behind his newly purchased house, with oddities and curious collectibles he had accumulated throughout his travels.   Stories of Shepard's pranks, accounts of his farfetched experiences, and tours through his extraordinary den entertained locals, business guests and tourists alike. Shepard often cooked for his business associates and friends, before sitting down to interesting conversation. The visits often concluded with Shepard presenting his guests with a caricature of them drawn during their stay. These activities further increased Shepard's popularity and made his name known to people outside the lumber industry.[12]

In addition to his daily activities in Rhinelander and his constant cruising trips, Eugene Shepard took an active and leading role in promoting Oneida County through its annual county fairs. The display of progress coupled with ample opportunities to utilize his showmanship made Shepard a constant patron at fairs and exhibitions throughout the Midwest well before Oneida County held its first fair. Acting as an agent for a hotel company, Shepard was involved in marketing week-long stays in Chicago for the 1893 World's Fair and Columbian Exposition. In December of 1892, the Security Hotel Company of Minneapolis, Minnesota had recently completed a $100,000 Chicago hotel within six blocks of the World's Fair entrance. As the exposition opened early the following year, Shepard sold hotel reservations to the residents of Northern Wisconsin at ten dollars per week. Impressed by the accomplishments such displays of progress produced, and being a determined area booster, Shepard took an

---

[12] Holmes, <u>Badger Saints and Sinners</u>, 467.

active role in the Oneida County Fair from its inception.[13]

The first annual Fair and Exposition of the Oneida County Agricultural Society was held on September 7th, 8th, and 9th of 1896. The county constructed a clay half-mile horse track, a football field, a main exposition building, and grand stands on the newly designated fairgrounds in Rhinelander. Although the goals of the fair were later described as "an effort to advance the agricultural interests in Oneida County," in 1896 the agricultural output of the sparsely settled county was less than impressive. As a result, the fair organizers reserved the main building for the city's merchants instead of the county's farmers. The *New North* explained: "The farm product and livestock exhibit cannot be expected to be very extensive in a community where the agricultural interest has only commenced to be developed, but there will be a good showing made nevertheless." The drawing cards of the first fair included a football game between Rhinelander and Green Bay, and horse races that ran horses from as far away as Stevens Point, Wausau, Ironwood, Michigan and Minneapolis, Minnesota. But it was E.S. Shepard's recently captured hodag, housed in a dimly lit tent near the entrance gate, that made the fair memorable.[14]

The second annual county fair, spanned an extra day and saw the entertainment of the fair greatly expanded. The county added a midway complete with a five-cent-per-ride merry-go-round, a knife board, fair security and expanded agricultural exhibits. In 1897 Oneida County sent its first exhibit to the State Fair. Through the turn of the century the fair continued to grow and prosper, and

---

[13] New North, December 22, 1892, p.4.

[14] Vindicator, May 13, 1896, p.1, and September 10, 1896, p.1; Rhinelander Herald, September 5, 1896, p.1, and September 12, 1896, p.4; New North, May 14, 1896, p.1, June 4, 1896, p.1, and September 3, 1896, p.1. E.S. Shepard's hodag is discussed separately in chapter four.

Eugene Shepard, his energy and hodag, played an active part in its development. In 1903, however, Shepard took his role in the county fair a giant step further.[15]

The Eighth Annual Oneida County Fair and Agricultural Exposition opened on September 14th, 1903 with a speech from Governor La Follete followed by Japanese day fireworks. Fair patrons must have been impressed with the renovations of the fair grounds and especially the new exhibit constructed by Eugene Shepard. Shepard, working with several teams of horses and a crew of men had constructed an extravagant exhibit that displayed the beauty of Northern Wisconsin as he first experienced it as a timber cruiser. The exhibit, speckled with ferns, moss and trees native to Northern Wisconsin, housed an artificial lake that teamed with various species of fish which included a 48 1/2" muskellunge. A rustic bridge bisected the lake leading to a cruiser's log cabin, complete with an exterior stone chimney. Near the cabin, Shepard had constructed a bark wigwam and displayed "implements of war and trophies of chase." Eight Ojibwa Indians, including "a native fortune teller," were hired to dance for the fair patrons. Cooks fried, baked, stewed, boiled, and prepared beans in a "bean pit" (a practice Shepard had learned while cruising). Potatoes and other diverse dishes were also served, with Shepard overseeing the food preparation and doing much of the cooking himself.[16]

To defray the costs of constructing such an extravagant exhibit and paying his native dancers and hired cooks, Shepard charged an admission fee to his exhibit. Although Shepard claimed he hired "a rain god from Arizona" to stand on his head to ward off the rain, his

---

[15] New North, September 3, 1896, p.1.

[16] Ibid., September 10, 1903, p.1, and September 26, 1903, p.4.

efforts were to no avail. It rained hard the first two days of the fair. Although the last day saw the largest single-day attendance in the fair's history, it could not offset the loss. The 1903 fair closed $600.00 dollars in the red, and Shepard himself lost a large quantity of money. That his attempt to display what he loved about Northern Wisconsin did not turn a profit seems to have had little impact. One local paper reported: "Gene did not play even when it came to figuring up the cost but he has no complaint to make." Not only did he not complain, but Shepard immediately began to expand his exhibit for the following year.[17]

A week after the close of the 1903 fair, Shepard announced that he recently purchased three badgers and that he intended to construct a twenty-five-mile-square game farm. In addition to the badgers, Shepard intended to stock the park with moose, deer, and other wild animals native to Northern Wisconsin. As the 1904 county fair opened, Shepard had expanded his exhibit and transported his growing game farm to the fairgrounds at a cost of $600.00. Shepard's actions during the 1903 and 1904 fairs and in the creation of his game preserve illustrate an interesting change in his conception of natural resources. In 1891 letters detailing his trips to Hannaford, Minnesota, Shepard spoke of shooting mass quantities of ducks that he later discarded. He also mentioned the killing of a bear and her two cubs for trophies and sport. By 1903, he was creating game farms and displaying animals at fairs so that others might enjoy what he had once taken for granted. Shepard always enjoyed hunting and continued to hunt and fish often, but in his later years it seems he became more aware of the importance and limited nature of the resources

---

[17] Ibid., September 26, 1903, p.1 and 4.

he harvested.[18]

Shepard had traveled throughout northern Wisconsin, Minnesota and Michigan before it was settled to any notable extent. He witnessed the coming of progress, settlement, and its inevitable side effects. That he welcomed and worked for progress, settlement, and advancement of Northern Wisconsin is certain. There is also sound evidence, seen through his own actions, that he began to respect what progress seemed to eclipse. Among other things, he began to refer to himself as a naturalist instead of a timber cruiser or real estate dealer. This emerging respect prompted many things in addition to his fair exhibits and game farm (the latter he eventually donated to Milwaukee's Washington Park Zoo). In these efforts, as in everything else he did, Shepard's humor permeated his actions. For example, he collected a pack of wolves which he promptly announced hunted other wolves. He also imported a pair of moose from Northern Minnesota, which he trained to pull him in his two-wheeled horse buggy. He explained that his moose could out-run any team of horses. Unfortunately, nobody but Eugene ever saw them exceed a lazy trot (see figure 3.4).[19]

Shepard also developed a fondness for race horses. In December of 1905, Eugene Shepard attended a Chicago horse sale with his son and purchased two well-bred horses. The first was a year-old bay filly named "Harmonia," but it was the second that became Shepard's prize possession. "Get-a-way," was a five-year-old Chestnut gelding trotter with an impressive pedigree who had once covered a mile in $2:12^{1/4}$ time. Bred in California, and previously owned by a rancher in Colorado,

---

[18] "To Establish Game Preserve," New North, October 1, 1903, p.1; New North, August 11, 1904, p.1; Shepard, "Big Fork Country," New North, December 17, 1891.

[19] "Wolves Hunt Wolves," New North, March 9, 1903, p.1.

Get-a-way quickly became the horse to beat in Northern Wisconsin. Years later, the horse's death devastated Shepard who had become extremely attached to the animal.[20]

Shepard's spending on his fair exhibits and hobbies suggests that he was not frugal with his money. The opposite is probably closer to the truth as Shepard made and lost several fortunes throughout his life. Always spending freely on entertainment, hobbies and living essentials, Shepard dispersed his income as fast as he earned it. One glowing example of his free-spending nature is the first Rhinelander dwelling Shepard erected. Upon his relocation to the new hamlet, he immediately erected an impressive dwelling for his family. Shepard's original Pelham Street homestead was completed in May of 1886, and he and his family moved in early the following month. The two story structure was later renovated and enlarged to 14 rooms. The family lived in the dwelling until 1906 and thereafter Shepard rented the structure as a boarding house. In January of 1911 Shepard sold the "splendid, centrally-located property" for $2,000.00.[21]

Possibly the best example of Shepard's extravagance was his 1905 purchase of a 61-foot pleasure boat. The boat's custom construction spanned nearly a year in Frank Sayner's Rhinelander factory, and was the largest and most spectacular vessel Sayner produced. The boat housed two cabins, a kitchen, a pantry, a bath and a toilet. The main cabin, located on the lower deck and used for dining and sleeping, measured 10'x16' and could sleep sixteen people. The second cabin, also on the lower deck, measured even

[20] New North, June 11, 1903, p.1, July 8, 1909, p.1, and September 16, 1909, p.1; Vindicator, January 3, 1906, p.4 and September 19, 1906, p.1; Shepard, Paul Bunyan, iv.

[21] New North, June 17, 1886, p.1, and March 25, 1886, p.1; "Excellent City Property Sells," New North, January 12, 1911, p.1.

larger at 10'x22'. The upper deck housed a detachable pilot's house (to facilitate rail transport) capable of seating ten and additional sleeping quarters for six people. A thirty-horsepower Fairbanks gasoline engine, disguised as a steam engine and capable of producing "puffs of smoke up the stack," powered the sternwheel boat. An engine-heated hot water system, electric lights, and a log (speedometer) equipped the boat. For the peace of mind of its passengers, the boat carried 24 life preservers, three rowboats and was manned by a three-man crew: an engineer, helmsman, and cook. According to Jack Cory, "On the deck and standing guard was a ferocious black Hodag, spikes and claws ready for action." On either side of the bow was the boat's name painted in script: *S.S. Hodag.*[22]

Originally Shepard intended to transport the boat by rail to Saint Paul, launch it on the Mississippi River and make the trip to Saint Louis for the 1905 St. Louis Exposition and World's Fair. Shepard intended the maiden voyage as a publicity trip boosting the opportunities available in Northern Wisconsin. In addition, he wished to show the passengers, largely Oneida County school teachers, a good time free of charge. For the occasion Shepard outfitted the boat with "a full service of cut glass and sterling silver." Each piece of silverware was custom made with "Hodag" inscribed in cursive. Unfortunately, the boat's completion was delayed and it never made the St. Louis trip. Instead, Shepard launched the *S.S. Hodag* in early April of 1905 upon the waters of the Wisconsin River via Boom Lake. Although the *Vindicator* announced "the boat scarcely draws 20 inches of water and will, it is thought, be able to go several miles up the stream," the

---

[22] "Shepard's Boat Launched Apr. 10," Vindicator, April 12, 1905, p.1; Joy Vancos, "The Rhinelander Boat Company: The Early Years," Our Town (Rhinelander, Wisconsin), May 21, 1995, section 2, p.1; Cory, Jack Cory's Scrap Book, 93.

boat was indeed too large for the northern portions of the Wisconsin River and unable to navigate the shallow waters. In addition, the boat was too tall to pass under the bridges that crossed the upper Wisconsin. The maiden voyage of the *S.S. Hodag* proved to be one of its last, and the boat rotted on the shoreline of Boom Lake. The *S.S. Hodag* cost Shepard over $5,000.00 in real estate trade and today remains one of the best examples of his extravagance and, in many respects, his foolishness.[23]

Shepard's actions in early 1906 further serve to emphasize his free-spending nature. Having completed an extremely profitable cruising trip throughout the West Coast in late 1905, Shepard engaged in a massive spending spree the following year. He purchased the most elaborate residence in Rhinelander, two lots in the Rhinelander's down-town business district, two well-bred race horses, a "fine regulation combination billiard and pool table" for his youngest son Layton, and took his wife and Layton, on a three-month vacation to California. He did this in addition

---

[23] "Shepard's Boat Launched," Vindicator, April 12, 1905, p.1; Cory, Jack Cory's Scrap Book, 93; Holmes, Badger Saints and Sinners, 465; "Fate of Terrible Hodag Cleared Up At Last," p.5. See also: Gard and Sorden, Wisconsin Lore, 253; and "The Hodag," New North, April 13, 1905, p.1. The Rhinelander Historical Museum owns an original sterling-silver spoon from the *S.S. Hodag's*. In the article "Hoax Alive and Well: Hodag Fooled Some People For A Time," Wisconsin Then and Now reports that Shepard "shelled out $13,000 for a large boat...and spent another $9,000 fitting it out..." This is undoubtedly a greatly exaggerated sum as contemporary accounts state that Shepard paid only $8,500 for the purchase of "The Pines," in 1906. Additionally, Fred Holmes and the 1923 Sentinel Sunday Magazine both report the boat was purchased and outfitted for just over $5,000. See chapter five for a discussion of the "Hodag Bell," as a high school football trophy.

to funding his failed campaign for the State Assembly.[24]

The best example of the immoderation of Shepard's 1906 spending spree was the purchase of "The Pines." In early January 1906, Shepard purchased E.M. Kemp's summer home. Kemp, a wealthy industrialist and the former proprietor of the Wabash Screen Door Factory, had erected an extraordinary residence just south of the city proper at the confluence of the Pelican and Wisconsin Rivers. Ironically, the structure stood on the very area where Shepard and A.A. Webber camped during their 1870 cruising trip. Shepard paid $8,500 for the property which the *Vindicator* called "one of the most desirable pieces of property in the city." The residence, which later included brick structures which served as a barn and Shepard's extravagant den, was dubbed "The Pines" and became one of the most impressive homes in the city (see figures 3.5-3.7).[25]

At times Shepard was well off and sound financial management could have certainly made his life very comfortable. His unbounded extravagance, however, often left him in financial difficulty. That he was unable to serve as a financial backer of the paper mill in 1903 or the development of Hat Rapids into a power plant in 1904, suggests that he experienced financial difficulties. Both projects were developments that Shepard strenuously advocated in the decades prior to their realization. It is logical to assume that if he had the resources, he would have quickly invested in the two projects. Shepard's shaky

---

[24] With the exception of the house and the billiard table, these purchases have been described in different contexts in earlier chapters. They are brought up here to emphasize Shepard's free-spending nature. Shepard also ran for Rhinelander Mayor, but did not campaign or spend any money on this attempt. For an account of the purchase of the billiard table see: <u>Vindicator</u>, February 7, 1906, p.1.

[25] "Buys Kemp Home," <u>Vindicator</u>, January 3, 1906, p.5.

financial standing can be seen in other instances as well. For example, in 1911 he put his horse "Harmonia" up for collateral on a loan of $175.00 so he could take care of "a note at the bank and some expenses...at the court house." Shepard admitted that he was financially "hard up," when he put the horse, which he valued at $1,000.00, up for collateral. The specifics of the loan, which Shepard had secured from a friend, were ambiguous and later disputed. Shepard and the creditor, Joseph Hartley, ended up in civil claims court disputing the rightful ownership of the horse; Hartley was awarded custody.[26]

By 1909 the 56-year-old Shepard experienced financial difficulties and "his present and future earning capacity [was] somewhat problematical on account of broken health and ability."[27] By the end of his life Shepard was completely insolvent. Although he still owned several Rhinelander plats in addition to large tracts of land in Oneida and Vilas counties, his holdings were largely unproductive of income, and he was unable to pay the taxes. In September of 1922, before the Circuit Court of Oneida County, Shepard's second wife, Karretta Gunderson Shepard, alleged that her husband "has been for many years financially unable to care for and protect his title in said lands or to support himself..." His wife claimed that, at Shepard's request, she had used her "own individual and separate estate and income in the payment of taxes, redemption of tax certificates, clearing of title...and improvements of" her husband's properties. According to his wife, without her assistance Shepard would have "lost through outstanding taxes" all that he owned. The often quoted statement that "Shepard gained and lost several

---

[26] E.S. Shepard vs Joseph Hartley, Oneida County Circuit Court--Civil, Box #35, Volume #4, Case #1465, Filed August 25, 1911.

[27] Eugene Shepard vs Mildred Shepard, Case #1302.

fortunes in his lifetime" carries with it a large degree of accuracy. His extravagance in times of fortune coupled with his inability to adequately plan for the future, resulted in an extremely fluid financial situation that stagnated on extremes: exorbitant wealth or absolute poverty.[28]

Shepard's personality and character included desirable traits that allowed him to accomplish many of the things that made him famous. He had a great sense of humor and a flair for showmanship. Furthermore, he was intelligent, resourceful, and honest in his work (if not in his leisure). Unfortunately, Shepard's character also contained vices much more troublesome than his financial foolishness.

Existing evidence suggests that Shepard drank often and that at least some of his pranks were ill-fated results of this over indulgence. Even in the earliest days of Rhinelander's existence, it seems that alcohol played an important part in Shepard's life. Like many communities founded in the late nineteenth century, Rhinelander's founders established the hamlet as a "dry" city. Shepard explained how he and others side stepped the inconvenience of the city's prohibition ordinance:

> [If] a man was posted right up to date...he would sneak off by himself alone to Faust's hardware store open the door under the stairs and step inside when Mrs. Faust was not looking and draw a glass of something in the liquid form that tasted like corn juice, make a deposit of 10 cents on the head of the barrel and make his own change from what he found there by the dim light of a lantern hanging on a nail and listen very quiet for customers in the store and step out quickly and leave the premises like an honest man.[29]

---

[28] E.S. Shepard vs Carrie Shepard, Oneida County Circuit Court--Civil, Box #61, Volume #5, Case #2478, Filed September 19, 1922.

[29] Shepard, "Reminiscences," New North, December 12, 1912.

Rhinelander eventually repealed its ill-fated prohibition experiment, and saloons were allowed within the city limits. If his actions were any indication, it is plausible to assume that Shepard frequented these establishments. One New Year's night he drove his horse and buggy through downtown Rhinelander. Nearing the city's center, he turned his horse and buggy on the wooden sidewalks and scattered the pedestrians. After being stopped by a city police officer, Shepard explained: "I wanted to let the people know that I hadn't made a New Year's pledge to swear off drinking." In another instance, to force him to sleep off a drunk, Shepard's family took his clothes and locked him in an upstairs room. The captive tied the bed sheets together as a makeshift rope and escaped out the window. The following morning found Shepard sleeping nude in a downtown furniture store's window display. Although humorous after nearly one hundred years, Shepard's drunken exploits weighed heavy on his family.[30]

Other "pranks," although not necessarily induced by alcohol, were equally disturbing. In September of 1908, for example, Shepard invited two newly hired grade-school teachers to go for a Saturday tour of the city. The two teachers readily accepted the opportunity to be shown around their new home. Shepard picked them up in an open carriage pulled by two black horses. Nearing the conclusion of the tour, he took the teachers along Thayer Street to show them the city's sawmills. Crossing the railroad tracks, Shepard:

> dropped the reins over the edge and gave his wild yell, and the horses tore right down the tracks. The wheels on the right side went over the open rail. [One of the teachers] was thrown over the side of the carriage and the wheels passed

---

[30] Holmes, <u>Badger Saints and Sinners</u>, 469; Mary Shepard Kosloske interview, 29 February, 1996.

over her. She was very bruised.[31]

In another instance, Shepard played a prank on a close friend, Miles Boone. Shepard, in retaliation for a trick Miles had played on him, paid a Native American women to put her arm around his friend and get Boone to do the same. The women succeeded and Shepard took a picture of the embrace. He later went to Boone's house and purposely dropped the picture so that Mrs. Boone was sure to find it. The ploy worked and Boone's wife moved out of the house and made preparations to leave the city. Shepard let the prank develop for a week, at which time he finally explained to the distraught couple what had happened. In the case of the injured school teacher and the shaken marriage, as well as in many others, it is clear that Shepard's sense of humor was misguided and carried too far.[32]

Despite these drunken exploits and ill-fated pranks, it appears the general populace of Rhinelander, tolerated, if not enjoyed, Shepard's antics. Understandably, his family was not so forgiving. Shepard's personality, character traits, and flaws made his relationship with his family a volatile one at best. The ill effects of Shepard's drinking, constant pranking and life decisions affected his family more than it did his friends and acquaintances. Furthermore, he often neglected his family, expected them to partake in his ploys of foolery and promotion, and treated them with little or no consideration. Shepard's failed family life is by far the most disturbing feature of his biography.

Shepard's livelihood required that he be absent from his family often and for extended periods. After the family

---

[31] Mrs. Isabel Ebert as quoted in Gard and Sorden, Wisconsin Lore, 251.

[32] Shepard, Paul Bunyan, 48-50.

moved from New London to Rhinelander in 1886, Mildred, Claude and, after 1892, Layton, often returned to New London to spend extended periods with Mildred's parents. Often these stays spanned four or five months, and usually coincided with Eugene's cruising trips. For example, during Shepard's attempt at founding Hannaford his family spent long period in New London. Even when Eugene returned to Rhinelander, instead of spending time with his family he often went on fishing and hunting trips with his friends that lasted days or even weeks. As his sons grew older Shepard did indeed take a more active interest in them. Claude worked as a surveyor and often served as a member of his father's crew during his teen years. Likewise, as Layton grew older, Shepard occasionally took him along on business trips. In 1903, for example, Shepard took his youngest son on a business trip to Milwaukee and they extended their stay several days to hear President Theodore Roosevelt speak. Three years later, as alluded to earlier, Shepard took Mildred and Layton to California for a three-month vacation. Unfortunately, these instances of family involvement appear to be the exception. As a result, Shepard's two sons cultivated a close relationship with their mother that largely excluded their often absent father.[33]

Furthermore, Shepard's constant showmanship often asked too much of his family. The best example pertains to Shepard's most famous hoax, the hodag. In order to make the creature look realistic Shepard had his sons

---

[33] This information is derived from extensive reading of the New North's local news sections, which kept close tabs on the activities of E.S. Shepard and his family, from 1882 through 1923. For specific examples of the habits described see: New North, May 28, 1885, p.1, April 15, 1886, p.1, May 20, 1886, p.1, December 29, 1887, p.1, January 28, 1892, p.5, May 12, 1892, p.1, September 8, 1892, p.1, August 31, 1893, p.3, June 28, 1894, p.1, August 5, 1897, p.1, and April 2, 1903, p.5. See also: Eugene Shepard vs Mildred Shepard, "Findings of Fact," case #1302.

manipulate the movements of the creature through a system of wires, while he explained to the stunned onlookers the capture and habits of the beast. As the hodag gained popularity, the time requirements on his sons increased. In a 1963 interview, Layton explained the "downside" of the hodag ploy:

> To be quite frank, the Hodag was quite a painful thing to the family. Suppose you had a fellow like [Eugene] in your family and a constant stream of people coming? [sic] People would come in on the train and rush over and try to see that Hodag between trains. Can you imagine what a pain in the neck that would be?[34]

The requirements Eugene's showmanship added to his extensive absence and his abuse of alcohol severely undercut his relationship with his immediate family.

When Shepard began to cut back his cruising activity and spend more time in Rhinelander, his relationship with his family deteriorated even further. By 1907 the worsening situation convinced Mildred, Claude's family and Layton (all of whom lived at The Pines) to leave Eugene. In early August, 1907 Mildred initiated divorce proceedings before the Civil Court of Oneida County. In a sworn affidavit, Mildred alleged:

> That for the past several years...[Eugene] has practiced a course of cruel and inhumane treatment of...[her] , by using personal violence and other means, without cause or justification and in disregard of his marriage vows. That he has repeatedly laid violent hands on her, choked her, abused her and threw cold water on her, repeatedly calling her vile

---

[34] Layton Shepard interviewed by Gard and Sorden, 1963, tape recording, Waukesha, Wisconsin, as quoted in "Hoax Alive and Well," 3. I have been unable to locate the tape or transcription of this interview which accounts for much of the information in Gard and Sorden's Wisconsin Lore and Dave Peterson's Hodag: A New Musical.

names and otherwise misused her without cause or excuse. That as a result of this treatment...[she] has become sick, sore and in a nervous condition and has become in great fear of...[Eugene] and has been compelled to leave her home and take refuge with her friends.[35]

Mildred asked for custody of Layton, then 14, alimony and child support. The court ordered Eugene to provide for Mildred's court costs and her subsistence throughout the suit. Before the case was settled, Eugene convinced Mildred to drop the suit. Mildred, however, continued to reside with Claude's family.

By 1909, Eugene Shepard's relationship with his family had deteriorated to the point of not only animosity but outright violence. Eugene's live-in housekeeper became a point of contention; Mildred believed that her husband maintained an improper relationship with the women. In September, Eugene petitioned the court to issue restraining orders against Claude, Claude's wife Millie and Layton. Shepard charged the three with trespassing and theft of his personal property. In a different suit initiated the same month, Eugene sued Mildred for divorce. Eugene charged Mildred with treating him with "extreme cruelty since about the beginning of the year 1900." The family crisis had come to a head the preceding month. On August 24, 1909, after a argument over financial issues exploded, a noon luncheon became violent. Later court findings explained: "the quarrel developed into threats of and attempts at violence with chairs and other like weapons between...[the father] and the sons, whereupon the sons drove...[the father] from the house and pursued him for a

---

[35] Mildred Shepard vs Eugene Shepard, Oneida County Circuit Court--Civil, Box #27, Volume #3, Case #1155, Filed September 7, 1907. The words "choked her" are crossed out. This case and all others cited in this paper as held in "volume #3" are mis-indexed at the Oneida County Courthouse. Although my citations are in conflict with the index they are accurate.

considerable distance." In Shepard's sworn complaint, he claimed that, acting on the urging of his mother, Claude had chased him from the house "armed with a heavy ironed stake." Eugene alleged that previously Mildred attempted to persuade her sons to kill him. Mildred, Eugene insisted, "loaded a revolver and gave...[it] to...Layton...and then and there directed him to kill his father." Furthermore, Eugene accused Mildred of trying to poison him repeatedly, causing great financial loss by interfering with his business dealings, and wrongly accusing him "of conduct in violation of his marriage obligations and...of associating with lewd women."[36]

Mildred, denying each of Eugene's claims, filed a counter-suit for divorce. She stated that Eugene instigated the divorce only because he knew that she was about to do the same. In addition, Mildred re-issued her 1907 complaints. The court listened to two days of testimony and ruled without a jury. The court found that Eugene was "rough and ready, eccentric and unconventional," while Mildred was "an intelligent and educated women who observes social customs and amenities;" that:

> the parties are very unlike, in fact nearly the direct opposite in taste, habits of thought and ideas of proper course of life. That each possessed a temper that is easily aroused and becomes violent and unyielding when aroused. That when aroused...[Eugene] becomes violent and reckless in actions and language and...[Mildred] is resentful, fault finding and imperious. That when not in temper both are affectionate and [Eugene] is of a generous disposition... That...[Mildred] has been much inclined to humor and spoil her children while...[Eugene] when at home has been disposed to discipline and some hardship. That the Children have sided with the mother...and...have been the cause of much trouble between

---

[36] Eugene Shepard vs Claude Shepard et al., Oneida County Circuit Court--Civil, Box #30, Volume #3, Case #1300, Filed September 15, 1909; Eugene S. Shepard vs Mildred Shepard, Case #1302.

the parents... That all affection between the parties...has been utterly destroyed and instead thereof there is a great bitterness...[37]

The court concluded in favor of Mildred, finding:

That the conduct of...[Eugene] toward...[Mildred] has constituted inhuman treatment... That while...[Mildred's] treatment of...[Eugene] has been exasperating and not in accordance of her duties as a wife it has not amounted to cruel and inhuman treatment...[38]

The court awarded custody of Layton to Mildred, ordered Eugene to settle all of the court costs of both parties and provide for his ex-wife and son. The case was concluded on March 30, 1910, but difficulties arose over the valuation of Eugene's property requiring further proceedings. The suit was finally concluded on June 28, 1911.[39]

In mid July of 1911, just weeks after his divorce was finalized, Eugene Shepard remarried. While in Green Bay in the midst of a drunken stupor, Eugene, then 57 years old, married Karretta "Carrie" Gunderson, 25 years his junior. Shepard had only recently made the acquaintance of Carrie, and the marriage seemed to be entered into as much to upset Mildred as to please Eugene. Upon their return to Rhinelander the new couple repeatedly passed by Claude's house as Eugene yelled to his ex-wife: "Hey Molly, look what I got!" referring to his young bride. The cruelty of Shepard's actions emphasized his lack of consideration for his ex-wife and his two sons. It also illustrated the utter ruin of his relationship with his kin, his

---

[37] Eugene Shepard vs Mildred Shepard, "Findings of Fact," Case #1302.

[38] Ibid., "As Conclusions of Law," Case #1302.

[39] Ibid., Case #1302.

bitterness and that he had completely failed as a family man. Although his second marriage spanned more than a decade, that too ended in bitterness and resentment at the close of his life.[40]

Eugene S. Shepard remains, most definitely, one of Rhinelander's most eccentric, peculiar, notable and infamous citizens. Fred Holmes seemed to have a grasp on Shepard's personality as he reflected: "Gene Shepard was a queer combination of community jester and shrewd businessman... He was a showman, strayed from the circus lot, who did uncommon things." Shepard had a notorious sense of humor, was a fabulous storyteller, a prankster, a naturalist, and played a major role in the founding and perpetuation of the Oneida County Fair. He was also, however, extravagant and financially shortsighted. He drank heavily, carried his pranking too far and, sadly, he failed as a husband and father. He made some poor personal decisions and did some very questionable things; he hurt those who were closest to him. When evaluated as a whole, E.S. Shepard (good aspects and bad, desirable traits and character flaws) became a part of Rhinelander, its local color, and its history.

---

[40] Marry Shepard Kosloske interview, February 29, 1996; United States Federal Census, Rhinelander, Oneida County, 1920; E.S Shepard vs Corrie [sic] Shepard, Case #2478.

Figure 3.1: Drawing by Eugene Shepard. Shepard
and Shepard, *Paul Bunyan, iv.*

Figure 3.2: Drawing by Eugene Shepard. Shepard and Shepard, *Paul Bunyan*, 35.

Figure 3.3: Drawing by Eugene Shepard. Shepard and Shepard, *Paul Bunyan*, 51.

Figure 3.4: Eugene Shepard and his trained Moose, circa 1896. Rhinelander District Library Collection.

Figure 3.5: "The Pines," shortly after a July, 1910 tornado. Rhinelander District Library Collection.

Figure 3.6: "The Pines," February, 1996.

Figure 3.7: Shepard's Barn and Den, February, 1996.

CHAPTER IV

LONG LIVE THE HODAG

A combination of Eugene Shepard's experiences and character traits resulted in his most famous hoax, the "capture" and popularization of the hodag. Through the hodag Shepard displayed his intimate knowledge of the lumber industry and its occupational folklore, attempted to promote Rhinelander and Northern Wisconsin, and illustrated his flair for story telling, his showmanship, and his humor. Although other aspects of Shepard's eccentric persona have been discussed in newspaper articles and local publications, they have, without exception, been mentioned only briefly within the context of his hodag. Nineteen-ninety-six marks the hundred-year anniversary of the Rhinelander hodag's capture, and, although the actual hoax has long since been discarded, the hodag has not disappeared from Rhinelander.

Logically, this chapter should commence with a detailed description of the hodag's "authentic capture narrative." Unfortunately, like all of Shepard's Bunyan stories, if not lumberjack folklore in general, the hodag lacks a definitive creation account. With each telling of the story, by Shepard or others who retold stories of the mythical beast, the details change. Integrated with this legend, however, are actual events that did indeed occur. First, in 1896 Shepard and Luke "Lakeshore" Kearney created the hodag. Second, Shepard presented the hodag as a living creature at Northern Wisconsin county fairs and at his home.   Third, after exposing the hoax, Shepard continued to exploit his hodag in Rhinelander, Star Lake and at county fairs.

By the end of the nineteenth century the hodag legend had emerged as part of Northern Wisconsin lumberjack lore. Eugene Shepard probably did not invent the hodag legend, but rather only exploited it. In any event, that the legend existed well before Shepard "captured" the beast is a certainty. Originally the word "hodag" was used in the lumber camps as a slang reference for a "grub hoe or a maddox." By the time Shepard wandered the Midwest's woods, however, the term took on another meaning: a beast that emerged from the ashes of a cremated lumber ox. Lumberjacks used oxen to transport timber to navigable water routes or railroad spurs. As a result, the lumber ox's life was so demanding that it rarely lived longer than six years. Not only were these "beasts of burden" assigned the most difficult task of the trade, but they also endured the most abuse from their drivers. The oxen endured all the profanity the crass lumberjacks could dish out. Consequently, the woodsmen believed that a dead ox must burn for seven years (longer than it had lived) to cleanse its soul from the profanity it had known in life. So when an ox died the lumberjacks set the carcass atop a large brush pile and cremated the remains. From the ashes, the cremators believed, emerged the soul of the ox in a vile and vengeful form: a hodag.[1]

---

[1] Snake Editor [Eugene Shepard], "Capture of the Hodag," New North, October 28, 1893, p.2; Olsen, Our First Hundred Years, 98; Peterson, Hodag: A New Musical, 48. Any publication that mentions E.S. Shepard will have some discussion of the hodag. See the second note in the introduction and the bibliography for a general, although not definitive, listing. For the best and earliest accounts see: Shepard, "Capture of the Hodag," (cited above); "Black Hodag For Fair," New North, August 27, 1896, p.1; "Mid Virgin Forests," Chicago Evening Post, August 18, 1900, p.4; Kearney, Hodag, 9-17.

Shepard's earliest descriptions of a hodag described the animal as a 185-pound, seven-foot-long lizard-like beast. Its head was disproportionately large for its body with two horns growing from its temples, large fangs and green eyes. The body was stout and muscular, its back was covered with spikes which led to a powerful tail. The four legs were all short and sturdy with three large claws facing forward and one pointing the opposite direction. Short black hair covered the captured hodag, although Shepard pointed out that the beast "assumes the same color as the ox" who bore it, and that the black variety was just one of many. At times a hodag's nostrils shot flames and smoke and it always emitted a horrible odor described as "a combination of buzzard meat and skunk perfume." Having an extremely unsavory disposition, a hodag was "a terrible brute...assumes the strength of an ox, the ferocity of a bear, the cunning of a fox and the sagacity of a hindoo snake, and is truly the most feared animal the lumbermen come in contact with (see figures 4.1-4.3)."[2]

In October of 1893, Eugene Shepard, writing for the *New North* in his position as "Snake Editor," recounted the first unsuccessful attempt at capturing a live hodag. Armed with "heavy rifles and large bore squirt guns loaded with poisonous water," a group of lumberjacks set out to confront the beast recently discovered living near Rhinelander. After the hodag "scattered about the place" small fragments of the dogs the search party sent in to corner the beast, the hunters began to discharge their weapons in its direction. Their weaponry proved of little value and the hunters were forced to employ more drastic measures. Piling birch brush around the now irate

---

[2] [Shepard], "Capture of the Hodag," New North, October 28, 1893, p.2; "Black Hodag for the Fair," New North, August 27, 1896, p.1; "Mid Virgin Forests," Chicago Evening Post, August 18, 1900, p.4; Gerald Carlstein, "The Beast That Will Not Die," Wisconsin Trails 20, no. 2, (1979), p.30. The "Hindoo snake" was also a mythical beast of lumberjack lore.

creature, the lumberjacks lobbed sticks of dynamite at their prey. The explosions ignited a fire that engulfed the monster and eventually took the hodag's life. Before expiring the monster thrashed about widely for nine hours felling trees in every direction and putting the lives of its adversaries in grave danger. The charred remains of the beast were then allegedly brought to Rhinelander and exhibited.[3]

Several months later, in January of 1894, Andy W. Brown invented a log hauler he christened the *Hodag*. A.W. Brown, the fellow timber cruiser and lifelong friend of E.S. Shepard, created a steam-driven machine that replaced the role of the oxen in transporting timber. The name, of course, carried with it a special significance. By replacing the oxen, the log hauler made obsolete the beasts whose souls became hodags. Unfortunately, the working parts of the machine had previously been utilized by another entrepreneur and A.W. Brown's *Hodag* was denied a patent. Although the *New North* credited Brown with "immortalizing the Hodag," steam-driven log haulers, which eventually replaced oxen, never became known as *Hodags*. The burden of immortalizing the beast passed from A.W. Brown to his friend E.S. Shepard.[4]

Despite Brown's efforts, for the next couple years the hodag remained nothing more than lumberjack lore. In 1896, however, E.S. Shepard adapted the legend into a

---

[3]   [Shepard], "Capture of the Hodag," New North, October 28, 1893, p.2. This article gives no indication of the "Snake Editor's" identity, and is the only article I have discovered attributed to such an editor. An October, 1903 New North article, however, stated in reference to Shepard: "He occupies the position of Snake Editor in this office..." See: "To Establish a Game Preserve," New North, October 1, 1903, p.1.

[4]   "Hodag Hauler," New North, January 18, 1894, p.1. E.S. Shepard and A.W. Brown were first acquainted while timber cruising near Pelican Rapids (present-day Rhinelander) in the 1870s.

ploy that transcended the lumber camps. Concerned about
the lack of a drawing card for the first annual Oneida
County Fair, its management approached Shepard for some
guidance.   The latter, already known for his sense of
humor, affinity for pranks and flair for showmanship,
endeavored to create a drawing card. Over a span of four
months, Shepard, in cahoots with Luke "Lakeshore"
Kearney and possibly others, carved the hodag from a
peculiar-looking stump. The conspirators covered their
creation with the hide of a young ox and fitted it with the
horns of more mature cattle. A little over a week before
the fair was slated to open, Shepard announced, via the
front page of the *New North*, that he had captured a hodag
and intended to exhibit the beast at the upcoming fair. The
article briefly described the details of the capture which
occurred just northeast of Rhinelander on "the muddy bank
of Lake Creek, on Sec. 37, Town 37, Range 9 East."[5] The
hodag, caught by surprise in his den by a group of
lumberjacks, fell victim to a heavy dose of chloroform that
rendered it unconscious. Transported by wagon to the
Rhinelander fairgrounds, the lumberjacks confined the
hodag to a pit resembling its den "in order that the animal
would not discover the deception being practiced upon
him."[6]

Shepard displayed his captured beast in a dimly lit
tent near the entrance gate of the fair. On Monday and
Tuesday, the first two days of the fair, "the tent was filled

---

[5] The careful reader should have been skeptical from this
description of the location, as townships have only 36 sections.

[6] "Mid Virgin Forests," Chicago Evening Post, August 18,
1900, p.4; "Black Hodag for the Fair," New North, August 27,
1896, p.1. Luke Kearney published a short book entitled: The
Hodag and Other Tales of the Lumber Camps (Wausau, Wisconsin,
1928), in which he forwards a fundamentally altered capture
narrative. This publication has been cited several times in the
preceding pages.

with a crowd of curious people throughout the day." On Wednesday, "a large number gave up their dimes to see this strange animal and hear its history as told by Shepard himself." It is said that Shepard, through admission charges and the sales of pictures, took in $500.00, but this seems a bit exaggerated (see figure 5.2). In any event, Shepard kept the crowds a good distance from his monstrosity and separated the spectators from the curiosity with a curtain. The distance, inadequate lighting and the brief period spectators were allowed to view the hodag all contributed to a prevailing sense that it was indeed a living specimen. To further convince the spectators, Shepard's sons manipulated the bogus animal through a system of hidden wires. Shepard later recalled of the people who came to see his hodag: "as a rule, they were and are, intelligent and well informed people." But few, if any of the visitors thought the beast a farce in its first years of existence. From this introduction to the public, Shepard took his hodag to Antigo for the opening of the Langlade County Fair the following week. Throughout the turn of the century Shepard's hodag became a regular attraction at Northern Wisconsin county fairs and, in at least one instance, at the Wisconsin State Fair.[7]

In addition to displaying the hodag at county fairs, Shepard also showcased the peculiar beast at his Pelham Street home. Enticing train passengers as he traveled back to Rhinelander, Shepard often convinced the travelers to layover in the city long enough to catch a glimpse of the hodag. Nearing his home Shepard yelled out to his sons: "Boys, make sure the hodag is tied up so he doesn't get loose!" The instructions served as a signal to Layton and Claude to slip into the hodag's shed before the visitors entered. Hidden by bales of hay, the boys moved the

[7] "Shepard's Hodag," Rhinelander Herald, September 12, 1896, p.4; Shepard and Shepard, Paul Bunyan, 12; Vindicator, September 16, 1896, p.1.

animal through its system of wires, supplied growls and moans, and rattled the chain-linked fence which supposedly restrained the monstrosity. As at the fair, the environment, through Shepard's use of distance, poor lighting, and a curtain, further altered the visitors' perception. It is said that many of the travelers believed they had seen a living hodag.[8]

Of the thousands of people who came to view the hodag, oral tradition holds that P.T. Barnum was among them. The New York entertainer allegedly viewed the beast momentarily and immediately offered Shepard an exorbitant sum of money for the rights to display it. Shepard, of course, refused the generous offer. Some accounts report Barnum sent an agent to view and purchase the rights to the beast, while most maintain that the trickster himself made the trip from New York to Rhinelander. In these later accounts Barnum became one of the suckers he maintained were born every minute. If the "humbugger" traveled to Rhinelander, the trip was never mentioned by Barnum, or any of the chroniclers of his life. It is possible that his failure to detect the hoax caused him embarrassment and convinced him to omit the trip from his biography. It seems more likely, however, that the trip never occurred and that Shepard and others in Rhinelander concocted the story to further exploit the hodag.[9]

---

[8] Margery Peters of Rhinelander, Wisconsin, interviewed by author, 13 March, 1996, Telephone call from Sugar Camp, Wisconsin to Rhinelander, Wisconsin. Margery Peters is a close friend of the Shepard family. In childhood, her mother lived across Pelham Street from Eugene Shepard and his family. This story was derived from Margery's mother.

[9] Several publications mention P.T. Barnum's visit. For the most developed see: "Fate of Terrible Hodag Cleared Up at Last," The Sentinel Sunday Magazine, May 27, 1923, p.5. Carlstein in "The Beast That Will Not Die," questions this claim.

Like Barnum's involvement with the hodag, the Smithsonian Institute also allegedly showed interest in Shepard's hoax. After hearing reports of the hodag, the Smithsonian dispatched a team of scientists to investigate the mysterious creature. Supposedly, this inquiry forced Shepard to reveal the hoax and let the scientists inspect the creature without the distortion on which Shepard relied to perpetuate the ploy. The archives of the Smithsonian, according to Gerald Carlstein, fail to reveal any interest the museum might have taken in the hodag. In this regard the allegations that the Smithsonian sent scientists to investigate the hodag falls in the same category as the P.T. Barnum story: possible, but unlikely. In any event, the hodag ploy was uncovered and revealed to be a hoax before the turn of the century. The creature continued, however, to attract interest and visitors from every part of the country. That the hodag was not real seemed to have little, if any, effect on its popularity.[10]

During the summer of 1900, Shepard used the hodag, already revealed as a hoax, to solicit vacationers from Milwaukee and Chicago to his Star Lake resort. An article appearing in the *Chicago Evening Post*, written by someone well acquainted with Shepard (if not penned by Shepard himself), advertised the House of the Good Shepard via a detailed description of the hodag narrative. During that summer, Shepard kept the hodag at his Ballard Lake resort and displayed the caged beast to his guests. Interestingly, the article, even at this early stage in an account coming from Shepard himself, changed the details of the story. In the description published in the 1896 *New*

---

[10] Carlstein, "The Beast That Will Not Die," p.30. The interest of the Smithsonian is mentioned in several accounts of the hodag legend, and usually serves as the reason the hoax was revealed. The exact date the hoax was revealed is not known with any certainty. An August, 1900 article in a Chicago paper states "Since then [1896] Shep has fessed up." See: "Mid Virgin Forests," <u>Chicago Evening Post</u>, August 18, 1900, p.4.

North article, Shepard stumbled across the hodag while out for his evening stroll near Rhinelander. In the *Chicago Evening Post* article, Shepard discovered the hodag while on an extended cruising trip near Star Lake. Asleep in a cruising cabin, Shepard dreamt the scratching, moaning and howling of a strange animal awoke him. The "fierce shrieks and howls [were unlike]... anything Shepard ever heard." The next morning the cruiser awoke to discover strange tracks leading away from his cabin door. The curious woodsman decided to follow the tracks "for he was half inclined to believe his experience was not wholly a dream." Trailing the beast for three days and nights, he finally came to its den. The article is vague in its description of the actual capture, only briefly concluding: "after a desperate struggle the creature was made a captive." Plainly, this second account is strikingly different from the one first printed in the Rhinelander newspaper. Evolving details became the norm - repeated with every telling of the hodag narrative.[11]

Just as the early narratives of the hodag contradicted each other, so did most, if not all, of the details surrounding the legend. The origin, capture, description and habits of the hodag all continually changed. In addition to being the reincarnated ox spirit, the hodag was also described as "the missing link between the ichthyosaurus and the mylodoan," two prehistoric creatures. Closely related to its origin were the changing details of the hodag's capture. A second widely retold account of the capture insisted that Shepard acquired the beast by digging a large pit and then baiting the hodag into it. In the 1960s, Dave Peterson adopted this second version in a song sung from Shepard's perspective:

...I figured a way for catchin the beast; I dug me a great big

---

[11] "Mid Virgin Forests," <u>Chicago Evening Post</u>, August 18, 1900, p.4.

pit
You know--like they used to catch elephants in; only bigger by
quite a bit

Now that Hodag'll only eat bulldogs; So I got me a pair for
bait
Then I sat 'em across on the opposite side; And then I sat
down to wait

When the Hodag smelled them bulldogs; He came tearin'
through the trees
And the closer he came the less I heard; With the bangin' of
my knees

Then he spotted them bulldogs across the pit; And it looked
like he'd have em yet
But as he crossed that hole--down he went; And I got myself
a pet![12]

Both of the origin and capture embellishments were
detailed by Shepard's co-conspirator, Luke Kearney, in his
1928 book, *The Hodag and Other Tales of the Lumber
Camps*. That Kearney was a close friend of Shepard and
intimately involved with the creation of the hodag suggests
that Shepard was aware, if not the perpetuator, of these
embellishments.   In fact, the hodag legend is so
contradictory that it is extremely difficult to describe its
evolution.   The size and color of the hodag constantly
changed.   The hodag's eating habits were variously
described as comprised of "mud turtles and water snakes,"
oxen, human flesh and, in the most popular accounts,
"white bulldogs eaten only on Sundays." Furthermore, it
is not certain how many hodags Shepard actually captured.
Although he carved only one, he often insisted that he
captured a male and a female in addition to a baker's dozen
of eggs.   If nothing else, the "legend" of the hodag

---

[12] Peterson, Hodag: A New Musical, 48-49.

certainly lived.[13]

It is unclear what became of the captive hodag, but most local historians maintain that a fire destroyed the carved beast sometime after the turn of the century. Often it is said the hodag died in a fire that leveled the House of the Good Shepard on Ballard Lake. The date of this conflagration is quoted by various sources as sometime during the first decade of the twentieth century. Shepard, however, sold his resort in the autumn of 1900. It is possible that after Shepard sold his resort he maintained a summer cabin on Ballard Lake which might have burned and "killed the hodag." Like many things surrounding the hodag, the details of its death remain unclear. That a fire destroyed Shepard's creation, however, seems certain. In an article written shortly after Eugene Shepard died, his second wife confirmed the hodag was lost in a fire. Unfortunately, the article supplied no details. Since the passing of the first hodag, several Rhinelanderites carved replicas to replace it. The most recent carving remains on display at the Rhinelander Logging Museum.[14]

Shortly before the turn of the century, Shepard and a group of Rhinelander citizens posed for a picture with the hodag. The picture, a reenactment of the capture, became a popular postcard celebrating Rhinelander's most unique piece of local color. In 1952 another group of Rhinelander citizens posed for a new picture with a replica hodag (see figures 4.4 and 4.5). In 1973 the State Historical Society of Wisconsin erected a marker at the entrance of Rhinelander's Hodag Park to commemorate the legend of Shepard's beast (see figure 4.6). To this day the city and its high school tout the hodag as their official mascot. Although the ploy lasted but a few years, the legend of

---

[13] Kearney, The Hodag, 13-14.

[14] "Fate of Terrible Hodag Cleared Up At Last," The Sentinel Magazine, May 27, 1923, p.5.

Shepard's hodag has indeed endured.[15]

In addition to being the most interesting and unique aspect of Rhinelander's local color, the hodag comprises many facets of Eugene Shepard's biography. Combining lumber lore and practical pranking, Shepard endeavored to promote Rhinelander in his eccentric fashion. As with all his pranks (i.e., the rubber muskellunge and the scented moss) Shepard tried to turn a profit while exploiting the hodag. It seems, however, that his foremost goal in the creation of the hoax was to promote Rhinelander and Northern Wisconsin in an unusual fashion. Years later Shepard explained why he captured the Hodag:

> By no means is all the progress to be credited to the Hodag, but the Hodag did his bit! Not only hundreds, but thousands of people came to view the Hodag...and not one of them went away without having learned a little more about north Wisconsin and it is safe to guess that each one of those thousands told others what they had seen and heard and in this way the beauties, opportunities and resources of north Wisconsin spread, and many who came out of curiosity only, have come to make their home with us, either permanently or for a few weeks or months out of the year. Long live the Hodag![16]

In addition to amusing Shepard and others, the hodag brought people to Rhinelander. In doing so, the town promoters felt it fulfilled a crucial step in the process of booster-assisted city growth.

---

[15] Olsen, Our First Hundred Years, 101.

[16] Shepard, Paul Bunyan, 12.

BLACK HODAG

Figure 4.1: Shepard's first published drawing of a hodag appeared in the October 28, 1893 issue of the *New North*.

Figure 4.2: Shepard's hodag, circa 1899.
Rhinelander District Library Collection.

Figure 4.3: A nineteenth-century hodag postcard. Rhinelander District Library Collection.

Figure 4.4*: This 1899 photograph became the
popular "capture Postcard" during the 1920s.
Rhinelander District Library Collection.

*NOTE: According to an August 7th, 1952 article in the
Rhinelander Daily News, this picture was taken in 1899.
Eugene Shepard is standing to the far right holding a stick.
Mary Kosloske confirms that the boy lying in the
foreground is her father, Layton Shepard. In 1899 Layton
was seven years old.

Figure 4.5: A 1952 reenactment of the original "capture postcard." Rhinelander District Library Collection.

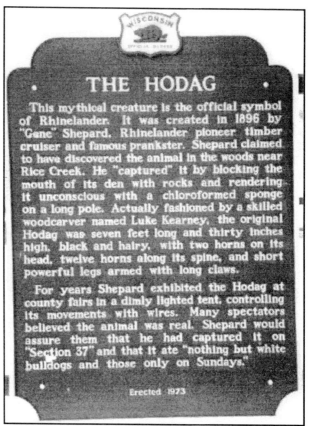

Figure 4.6: The State Historical Site Marker at the entrance of Hodag Park. Rhinelander, Wisconsin.

CHAPTER V

THE LIFE AND LEGACY OF EUGENE SIMEON SHEPARD

From Shepard's second marriage in July of 1911 to his death in March of 1923 he lived in virtual isolation from his family and the city with which he was so closely identified. Spending much of his time gardening at The Pines, Shepard had little or no contact with Mildred, Claude or Layton. He increasingly distanced himself from the civic affairs of Rhinelander. Shepard's health, problematic since 1909, severely hindered his ability to earn a living. To supplement his waning income, he rented rooms in his home and surrounding buildings to summer vacationers. By 1922 his second marriage had deteriorated to the point of separation. Eugene Shepard spent the last year of his life in poverty and isolation - sick in body and in mind (see figure 5.1 and 5.2).

As early as 1917, Shepard began to succumb to the worsening effects of his chronic illness and his 63 years. Speaking often of his gardening and the work it involved, he began to admit that his health had begun to affect his life. In a letter to an acquaintance dated July 3rd, 1917, Shepard complained: "I am working to [sic] hard. This morning I had to rool [sic] around on the floor a while [sic] to get limbered up so I could get to going." Three years later, his health deteriorated further as an infection in his right hip began to swell and cause chronic pain. Writing to another acquaintance during the summer of 1920

Shepard revealed: "I am getting old and timid... I am feeling some better in my legs this morning and got a fair sleep last night and I needed it badly for I had not slept much of any for about 20 days." The following years saw Eugene's health decline rapidly; he began to complain of lost vision, dilapidated mental condition, and severe pain. Two years later, Shepard described himself as "old and feeble and unable to earn a living."[1]

Shepard's ailing health convinced him to renovate The Pines into a sanitarium. Announcing his plans in September of 1922, Shepard hired the Chicago native Charles I. Kramer as the director. The two men believed the "up to date [*sic*] buildings and perfectly natural surroundings" were ideal for sanitarium purposes. In addition, Northern Wisconsin's "high altitude and pure air" would supposedly aid in the restoration of "health and vitality." The two devised plans to convert "one of the main buildings into the bath and treatment department." Although in private correspondence Shepard began to refer to his home as the sanitarium, it appears that the institution never opened to the public. Shepard's health declined rapidly immediately after he announced his plans to construct the sanitarium and he never completed the renovations.[2]

Shepard's inability to work, the strain of his sickness and the difficult financial situation adversely affected his marriage. In November of 1911, less than six months after Karretta and Eugene were married, Eugene deeded his wife several tracts of land in return for her

---

[1] Eugene Shepard to Mrs. Blencoe, July 3, 1917, E.S. Shepard Small Collection #1152, State Historical Society of Wisconsin; Eugene Shepard to Howard Stark, September 6, 1920, E.S. Shepard Small Collection #1152, State Historical Society of Wisconsin; Eugene S. Shepard vs Corrie [*sic*], Case #2478.

[2] "Sanitarium At Shepard's Pines," New North, September 7, 1922, p.1.

financial investment and help in the improvement and upkeep of his numerous real estate investments. On May 6th, 1922, Shepard, fearing his imminent death, deeded almost all of his real estate assets to his wife. According to Carrie Shepard, Eugene acknowledged that "the lands would have been lost through outstanding taxes," if it were not for the financial assistance and management of his wife. The following autumn, Carrie fell out of favor with Eugene and the latter began to regret his actions. On September 18, 1922 Eugene attempted to get the land transfers nullified in Oneida County Circuit Court. He claimed that when he signed the deed over to his wife the preceding May he suffered from a diminished mental capacity. He charged that his wife took advantage of his dilapidated mental state and "fraudulently prevailed upon him to execute and deliver to her a deed." Four days later, on September 24th, Eugene forced his second wife to leave their residence and reside with friends. Carrie Shepard responded to Eugene's charges the following month. Denying Eugene's allegations, Carrie explained that she had invested large sums of her own money for maintenance, upkeep and the payment of taxes. Nothing came of the action, and the court eventually dismissed the suit in 1948, long after both parties had died.[3]

On the 25th of November, 1922, Shepard again took his wife to court. This time he sued for divorce. He alleged his wife had stolen property, tax certificates, and money from him; pawned a $600 diamond from a ring he had given her; was "a women of a very violent temper and has frequently sworn at him and called him vile names;" like his first wife, attempted to poison him; "has...seriously neglected her house hold [sic] work;" has "refused to make his bed for weeks at a time and seldom cleaned his room;"

---

[3] E.S. Shepard vs Corrie [sic] Shepard, Case #2478; E.S. Shepard vs Carrie Shepard, Oneida County Circuit Court--Civil, Box #62, Volume #5, Case #2501, Filed January 3, 1923.

and, among other things, "associated with men and women of bad character and reputation and became intoxicated with them." Eugene ended his complaint by claiming that he was "extremely nervous and broken down in health and that he can no longer live with" his wife. He asked that the two be divorced and he retain the ownership of the deeded property. In regard to the disputed land titles, Carrie responded as she had in the previous case. In addition, she denied categorically each one of Eugene's allegations.[4]

In lieu of sending this case to trial, the court resolved the dispute by sanctioning a neutral trust arrangement. Trustees Alex McRea and S.D. Sutliff agreed to manage all disputed real estate. Both Eugene and Carrie received a $100.00 monthly stipend, and the trust supplied additional dividends if needed by either party for "maintenance, support, care, medical treatment... or nursing." If Eugene died prior to Carrie, all of his expenses and debts were to be paid and the remaining assets of the trust were to be delivered to Carrie. If Carrie died prior to Eugene, her heirs were to be paid $8,500 and the trustees were to continue managing affairs for the duration of Eugene's life. Although the court did not grant the divorce, it stipulated that each party "refrain from in any way molesting or annoying the other." It also issued an order "strictly forbidding each party from going to the abode of the other and from doing any and every act that may annoy or injure the other."[5]

As the stipulations of the trust arrangement suggested, Eugene Shepard was unsound in mind as well as body. He was also, from the summer of 1922 onward, completely isolated from his family, his second wife and the local community. Shepard spent the last year of his life

---

[4] Ibid., Case #2501.

[5] Ibid., Case #2501.

alone and deathly ill.   Three months before his death, writing to a friend in Madison, Wisconsin, Shepard summarized his unfortunate situation:

> I have been here sick alone ever since you was [sic] here and on the verge of utter dispondency [sic]. She [Carrie] has been awful mean to me. She is not allowed in the house at all. She Got in one day and looted it while she thought I could not live the day out... I have suffered awfully she has got some of my yellowed harted [sic] brother masons vamped and they have made me a lot of trouble. I am up this week most of the day and I am in hopes now to survive but had given it up as an imposibility [sic]... I have been sick & helpless most of the time but have got my eyesight mostly back again & am much improved but awful weak... My hart [sic] is now the weak spot.[6]

Clearly, the last three months of Shepard's life were not pleasant.

Shepard, afflicted with chronic nephritis, died at 11:00 pm on the 26th of March, 1923.   The death certificate recorded the immediate cause of as: "acute infection of the right leg and thigh." The next day, Carrie moved back into The Pines and began to make arrangements for the funeral. Across town, Mildred wept when she learned of Eugene's death.[7]

---

[6] E.S. Shepard to Mr. Nuzum, December 5, 1922, E.S. Shepard Small Collection #1152, State Historical Society of Wisconsin.

[7] Eugene S. Shepard, Death Certificate, c-1 830, #601, Oneida County, Wisconsin, March 24, 1923; Marry Kosloske interview, February 29, 1996. Claude and Layton Shepard sued Carrie Shepard and trustees Alex McRea and S.D. Sutliff shortly after their father's death. Their claim that the trust agreement be overturned because their father was of unsound mind when he agreed to it, was unsuccessful. All of Shepard's estate passed to Carrie Shepard, and upon her death in 1942 the estate was divided between Carrie's four nephews.

An unusual man died on March 26, 1923, but with that death, a common man passed as well. In addition to his impact on Rhinelander, we learn much about turn-of-the-century American history through the experiences of Eugene Shepard. Through his work as a timber cruiser, land agent and resident land speculator Shepard played a common role in the process of Midwestern land transfer. Although much of the financial benefits of Midwestern resources left the region as a result of federal land policies, Shepard's experiences illustrate that timber cruisers, land agents and resident land speculators also profited handsomely from the process of land transfer. Also related to his role as a woodsman, Shepard became familiar with the occupational lore of the lumberjacks and he contributed to it with his Paul Bunyan yarns. Likewise, Shepard's activities in voluntary booster organizations and his personal attempts to promote Rhinelander and Northern Wisconsin offer insight into turn-of-the-century community boosterism. In these endeavors and activities Shepard was not unique or extraordinary. Rather, he was one of many who carved a living from the land trade, contributed to lumberjack lore, and energetically boosted their community.

Shepard's impact on Rhinelander and Northern Wisconsin, however, is not ordinary. He combined two of his seemingly separate activities (use of lumberjack lore and community boosterism) into the hodag ploy that promoted the city. In addition to the hodag's success in attracting attention to Rhinelander at the turn of the century, the mythical beast accomplished much more. Shepard's hodag created a legacy in and around the city. Shepard played practically no role in the civic affairs of Rhinelander for the last fourteen years of his life. Almost immediately after his death, however, Eugene S. Shepard once again became closely identified with the city. Beginning slowly with his obituaries and growing sporadically through the years, Shepard's legacy, focusing primarily on his hodag, became a part of Rhinelander. His legacy, which is often the case with historical personalities, does not today mirror the entire reality of his life. The humor and oddities Shepard brought to the city and region are remembered, not his drinking, financial or family difficulties. Over the 73 years since Shepard died, the negative aspects of his biography have been largely forgotten, while the positive aspects have been enlarged and ingrained in Rhinelander's local color.

All the local papers carried front page obituaries of the eccentric early settler, but the *New North* paid the greatest homage. In an expanded article the paper stated:

> In the early development of Rhinelander and Oneida County Mr. Shepard took a prominent part. He was always a staunch supporter of any movement for public progress. Original in his ideas, he founded and promoted several clever advertising schemes which placed this city and county on the map. Chief among these was the "Hodag" a mythical animal... which attracted national attention for awhile... All told 'Gene Shepard was in a class by himself and his memory will linger long. Woodsman, artist, nature lover, story teller, and entertainer, he was undoubtedly one of the most unique personages to be found anywhere in the country.[8]

The paper was correct, Eugene Shepard's memory, via the hodag, did linger long.

By the end of the 1920s Rhinelander Hodag postcards were a common find around Northern Wisconsin. The high school adopted the hodag as the name of its yearbook and official mascot. In the 1930s Rhinelander sportswriters recovered the silver bell of Shepard's long-abandon *SS Hodag* and converted it into a high school football trophy. The bell, even today, serves as the prize for the winners of the annual Rhinelander/Antigo Wisconsin Valley Conference football game. Mimicking several college traditions, the bell is brought to the game

---

[8] "Life Closes For Eugene Shepard," New North, March 29, 1923, p.1.

and the victor is awarded possession until the following year (see figure 5.3).[9]

Furthermore, the Wisconsin Idea Theater produced a 1964 play entitled *Hodag: A New Musical Based on the Exploits of Gene Shepard, Wisconsin's Greatest Trickster.* The playwright, Dave Peterson, derived much of his narrative from material collected by Robert E. Gard and L.G. Sorden for their 1962 book *Wisconsin Lore.* Peterson also utilized a tape-recorded interview with Layton Shepard. The play opened in Rhinelander on July 18, 1964. The musical production traveled the state that summer, changed its name to *Who Wears the Pants*, and toured Europe, playing for American GIs, the following year. The play recounted Shepard's run-in with the Kentucky gunman, his ill-fated *SS Hodag*, and, of course, his hodag hoax. It also, however, portrayed Shepard as a town promoter rather than solely a pointless prankster. The citizens of Rhinelander received the play well, and it exposed a large segment of the population to the positive aspects of Shepard's character.[10]

Today, from Shepard Street to Hodag Park, Rhinelander continues to bear the mark of its most eccentric early settler. Currently no less than thirteen businesses have adopted Shepard's beast into their company titles. In fact you can buy a car at Hodag Auto, get its oil changed at Hodag Express Lube, fill it with gas at Hodag 76, and if you experience mechanical difficulties, call Hodag Towing to tow your new vehicle home. Additionally, every summer the music concert, "Hodag Country Fest," held at "Hodag Fifty" fairgrounds, is strenuously advertised over the airwaves of WHDG FM 97.5 - "Hodag County." Even the city police have bought into Shepard's gimmick; they proudly display a green

[9] Cory, Jack Cory's Scrapbook, 91-93.

[10] Peterson, Hodag: A New Musical.

hodag on the rear quarter panels of their squad cars (see figures 5.4-5.7). If the less-desirable aspects of Shepard's persona have been forgotten, the legacy of E.S. Shepard continues to thrive in Rhinelander. Exactly 100 years after Shepard captured Rhinelander's most peculiar booster, it seems appropriate to quote the unconventional woodsman in a centennial salute to his civic-boosting monstrosity: "Long Live the Hodag!"

Figure 5.1: Eugene S. Shepard, circa 1919.
Rhinelander District Library Collection.

Figure 5.2: Eugene S. Shepard, circa 1922.
Marry Kosloske Collection, Winchester, Virginia.

Figure 5.3: "The Hodag Bell," away from home at Antigo. March, 1996.

Figure 5.4: Rhinelander's city limits welcoming sign. August, 1995.

Figure 5.5: Hodag Park, Rhinelander Wisconsin. March, 1996.

Figure 5.6: Shepard Park is located in Rhinelander at the confluence of the Wisconsin and Pelican Rivers. August, 1995.

Figure 5.7: A Rhinelander Police car, decorated with hodags on its rear quarter panels. March, 1996

BIBLIOGRAPHY

PRIMARY SOURCES

Andreas, A.T. compiler. *History of Northern Wisconsin, Containing an Account of its Settlement, Growh, Development, and Resources; An Extensive Sketch of its Counties, Cities, Towns and Villages, Their Improvements, Industries, Manufactories; Biographical Sketches, Portraits of Prominent Men and Early Settlers, Views of County Seats, etc...* Chicago: Western Historical Company, 1881.

Fourteenth Census. Manuscript schedules of the fourteenth census, 1920. Rhinelander, Oneida County, Wisconsin. Microcopy. Madison, Wisconsin: State Historical Society of Wisconsin.

Lord, Alman I. *Industrial Review of Rhinelander, Wis.* Rhinelander, Wisconsin: Privately Printed, 1898.

"Mid Virgin Forests; Beauties and Attractions Found in Northern Wisconsin; Shepard and His Wonderful Hodag Which Hoodwinked the Natives and Others For Years." *Chicago Evening Post*, August 18, 1900.

New North. Rhinelander, Wisconsin. weekly. Selected Issues: December, 1882 through March, 1923.

Northwestern Lumberman. Chicago, Illinois. lumber industry weekly trade journal. Selected Issues: August, 1887 through January, 1892.

"Rhinelander." [in six parts]. *New North*, December 1, 1892 through January 19, 1893.

Rhinelander Daily News. Rhinelander, Wisconsin. Selected Issues: March, 1923 through May, 1995.

Rhinelander Herald. Rhinelander, Wisconsin. weekly. Selected Issues: August, 1896 through March, 1923.

Shepard, Eugene S. "A Trip to Hannaford." *New North*, March 22, 1894.

_____. "Big Fork Country." *New North*, December 17, 1891.

_____. "Boost Northern Wisconsin." *New North*, November 28, 1907.

_____. Death Certificate. Oneida County, Wisconsin. C-1, 830, #601. March 24, 1923.

_____. *Greatest Muskellunge Fishing In The World.* Promotional Handbill for the House of the Good Shepard. Star Lake, Vilas County, Wisconsin: Privately Printed, 1900.

_____. "Reminiscences of Eugene Shepard: Old and Well Known Citizen First Came Here Away Back in 1870." *New North*, December 12, 1912.

_____. to Judge A.H. Reid. n.d. reprinted in: "Mrs. Paul Bunyan Even More Resourceful Than Her Husband." *New North*, May 11, 1922.

_____. to Mrs. Blencoe. July 3, 1917. E.S. Shepard Small Collection #1152. Madison, Wisconsin: State Historical Society of Wisconsin.

_____. "To the Rainy River." *New North*, August 13, 1891.

_____. to W.E. Nuzum. December 22, 1922. E.S. Shepard Small Collection #1152. Madison, Wisconsin: State Historical Society of Wisconsin.

_____. v. Carrie Shepard. Oneida County Circuit Court--Civil. Box #62, Volume #5, Case #2501. Filed: January 3, 1923. Microcopy, Office of the Clerk of Court, Oneida County Court House. Rhinelander, Wisconsin.

_____. v. Corrie [*sic*] Shepard. Oneida County Circuit Court--Civil. Box #61, Volume #5, Case #2478. Filed: September 19, 1922. Microcopy, Office of the Clerk of Court, Oneida County Court House. Rhinelander, Wisconsin.

_____. v. Claude Shepard et al. Oneida County Circuit Court--Civil. Box #30, Volume #3, Case #1300. Filed: September 15, 1909. Microcopy, Office of the Clerk of Court, Oneida County Court House. Rhinelander, Wisconsin.

_____. v. Joseph Hartley. Oneida County Circuit Court--Civil. Box #35, Volume #4, Case #1465. Filed: August 25, 1911. Microcopy, Office of the Clerk of Court, Oneida County Court House. Rhinelander, Wisconsin.

_____. v. Mildred Shepard. Oneida County Circuit Court--Civil. Box #30, Volume #3, Case #1302. Filed September 22, 1909. Microcopy, Office of the Clerk of Court, Oneida County Court House. Rhinelander, Wisconsin.

Shepard, Eugene S., and Karretta Gunderson Shepard. *Paul Bunyan: His Camp and Wife.* Tomahawk, Wisconsin: By Karretta Gunderson Shepard, 1929.

Shepard, Mildred. v. Eugene S. Shepard. Oneida County Circuit Court--Civil. Box #27, Volume #3, Case #1155. Filed: September 7, 1907. Microcopy, Office of the Clerk of Court, Oneida County Court House. Rhinelander, Wisconsin.

Snake Editor. [Eugene S. Shepard]. "Capture of the Hodag." *New North*, October 28, 1893.

Twelfth Census. Manuscript schedules of the twelfth census, 1900. Arbor Vita, Vilas County, Wisconsin. Microcopy. Madison, Wisconsin: State Historical Society of Wisconsin.

Vindicator. Rhinelander, Wisconsin. weekly. Selected Issues: July, 1890 through March, 1923.

Warren, George Henry. *The Pioneer Woodsman As He Is Related To Lumbering In The Northwest.* Minneapolis: Press of Hahn & Harmon Company, 1914.

SECONDARY SOURCES

Ayers, Edward L. *The Promise of the New South: Life After Reconstruction.* New York: Oxford University Press, 1992.

Carlstein, Gerald. "The Beast That Will Not Die." *Wisconsin Trails* 20, no. 2 (1979): 29-30.

Cory, Jack. *Jack Cory's Scrapbook.* Lake Tomahawk, Wisconsin: Northland Historical Society, Incorporated, 1985.

Cronon, William. *Changes In The Land: Indians, Colonists, and the Ecology of New England.* New York: Hills and Wang, 1983.

_____. *Nature's Metropolis: Chicago and the Great West.* New York: W-W Norton and Company, 1991.

Derleth, August. *The Wisconsin: River of a Thousand Isles.* Madison, Wisconsin: The University of Wisconsin Press, 1942.

Ellerman, Cecelia M. *The Resort People.* Star Lake, Wisconsin: By the author, Box 94, 1989.

_____. *This Land The Way It Was (Sayner - Star Lake).* Star Lake, Wisconsin: by the author, Box 94, 1983.

"Fate of Terrible 'Hodag' Cleared up at Last!"   *The Sentinel Sunday Magazine*, May 27, 1923, p. 5.

Felton, Harold W. *Legends of Paul Bunyan*. New York: A.A. Knopf, 1947.

Gard, Robert E. and L.G. Sorden. *Wisconsin Lore*. Sauk City, Wisconsin: Stanton & Lee Publishers, Inc., 1980.

Gates, Paul Wallace. *The Wisconsin Pine Lands of Cornell University: A Study in Land Policy and Absentee Ownership*. Ithaca, New York: Cornell University Press, 1943.

"Hoax Alive and Well: Hodag Fooled Some People For A Time." *Wisconsin Then and Now* 22, no. 1 (August, 1975): 2-6.

Hoffman, Daniel. *Paul Bunyan: Last of the Frontier Demigods*. Philadelphia: Temple University Press, 1952.

Holmes, Fred L. *Badger Saints and Sinners*. Milwaukee, Wisconsin: E.M. Hale & Company, 1938.

Huston Harvey. *'93/'43 Thunder Lake Narrow Gauge*. Winnetka, Illinois: By the author, 860 Mount Pleasant Street, 1963.

Jones, George O. and Norman S. Mcvean, et al., eds. *History of Lincoln, Oneida, and Vilas Counties*. Minneapolis and Winona, Minnesota: H.C. Cooper, Jr. Co., 1924.

Kearney, Luke S. *The Hodag: And Other Tales of the Logging Camps*. Madison, Wisconsin: Democrat, 1928.

Kortenhof, Kurt Daniel. *Sugar Camp: The Origin and Early History of a Northern Wisconsin Community.* Eau Claire, Wisconsin: Heins Publications, 1993.

Kosloske, Mary, granddaughter of Eugene S. Shepard. Interviewed by author, February 29, 1996. Telephone call from Eau Claire, Wisconsin to Winchester, Virginia.

Mac Dougall, Curtis D. *Hoaxes.* New York: The Macmillian Company, 1921.

Mackay, Donald. *The Lumberjacks.* Toronto: McGraw-Hill Ryerson, 1978.

Nesbit, Robert. *Industrialization and Urbanization 1873-1893.* Vol. 3, *The History of Wisconsin.* Madison, Wisconsin: State Historical Society of Wisconsin, 1985.

_____. *Wisconsin: A History.* 2d ed. revised and updated by William F. Thompson. Madison, Wisconsin: University of Wisconsin Press, 1989.

Olsen, T.V. *Our First Hundred Years: A History of Rhinelander.* Rhinelander, Wisconsin: PineView Publishing, 1981.

_____. *The Rhinelander Country Volume Two: Birth of a City.* Rhinelander, Wisconsin: PineView Publishing, 1983.

Peters, Margery, friend of Shepard family. Interviewed by author. March 13, 1996. Telephone call from Sugar Camp, Wisconsin to Rhinelander, Wisconsin.

Peterson, Dave. *Hodag: A New Musical by Dave Peterson Based on the Exploits of Gene Shepard, Wisconsin's Greatest Trickster and Adapted From Material Collected by Robert E. Gard and L.G. Sorden.* Madison, Wisconsin: The Wisconsin Idea Theater [script available at the Mills Music Library, University of Wisconsin--Madison], 1964.

Rohe, Randall. "Star Lake: From Boom Town to Ghost Town." In *Proceedings of Seventeenth Annual Meeting of Forest History Association of Wisconsin, Inc.* Eagle River, Wisconsin, October 10-11, 1992, 37-45.

Ryan, J.C. "The Timber Cruiser." *Timber Bulletin* 40 (August/September, 1985): 27-29.

_____. "The Forgotten Cruiser." *Timber Bulletin* 47 (April/May, 1992): 30-31.

Smith, James Bruce. "The Movements For Diversified Industry in Eau Claire, Wisconsin, 1879-1907: Boosterism and Urban Development Strategy in a Declining Lumber town." M.A. thesis, University of Wisconsin--Madison, 1967.

Stark, William F. *Wisconsin, River of History.* By the author, 1988.

Stewart, K. Bernice and Homer A. Watt. "Legends of Paul Bunyan, Lumberjack." *Transactions of the Wisconsin Academy of Sciences, Arts and Letters.* 18, part 2 (1916): 641-667.

Vancos, Joy. "The Rhinelander Boat Company: The Early Years." *Our Town* (Rhinelander, Wisconsin) May 21, 1995, sec. 2, p.1.

ABOUT THE AUTHOR:

Kurt Daniel Kortenhof was raised in Sugar Camp, a small community seven miles north of Rhinelander, Wisconsin. He graduated from Three Lakes High School in May of 1989 and attended the University of Wisconsin at Eau Claire the following autumn. He earned his B.A. with a concentration in history in December of 1993, and his M.A. with a concentration in American social history in May of 1996. In addition to his studies at the University of Wisconsin at Eau Claire, Kurt has taken undergraduate coursework at the University of Alaska at Anchorage and graduate coursework at Villanova University in suburban Philadelphia. Currently he is a Ph.D. student in history at the University of Delaware. In addition to *Long Live the Hodag!*, Kurt published *Sugar Camp, 1891-1941: The Origin and Early History of a Northern Wisconsin Community* in 1993.

ORDERING INFORMATION:

Books by Kurt Daniel Kortenhof distributed by *Hodag Press*® include:

Kortenhof, Kurt Daniel. *Long Live the Hodag! The Life and Legacy of Eugene Simeon Shepard: 1854-1923*. Rhinelander, WI: Hodag Press, 1996. **$12.00**

Kortenhof, Kurt Daniel. *Sugar Camp, 1891-1941: The Origin and Early History of a Northern Wisconsin Community*. Eau Claire, WI: Heins Publications, 1993. **$10.00**

Please write directly to *Hodag Press*® indicating the title and number of copies desired. Make checks payable to *Hodag Press*® and add 5.5% sales tax to all Wisconsin orders (shipping is included in cover price). Discounts are available for bulk purchases and to booksellers.

Hodag Press®
5552 Jenny Webber Lake Road
Rhinelander, Wisconsin 54501